Thomas Merton

. . . *when speech is in danger*
of perishing or being perverted
in the amplified noise of beasts,
perhaps it becomes obligatory for
a monk to try to speak.

Seeds of Destruction

Thomas Merton
Social Critic

A Study by
James Thomas Baker

The University Press of Kentucky

for Jill & Jenji
who know and care

ISBN: 0–8131–1238–9

Library of Congress Catalog Card Number: 76–132827

Copyright © 1971 by The University Press of Kentucky

A statewide cooperative scholarly publishing agency
serving Berea College, Centre College of Kentucky,
Eastern Kentucky University, Kentucky State College,
Morehead State University, Murray State University,
University of Kentucky, University of Louisville,
and Western Kentucky University.

Editorial and Sales Offices: Lexington, Kentucky 40506

Contents

Preface   vii

Chapter One
    The Pilgrim's Progress   1

Chapter Two
    The World & Thomas Merton   27

Chapter Three
    The Social Ethics of Contemplation   44

Chapter Four
    The Battle of Gog & Magog   66

Chapter Five
    The Grim Reaper of Violence   98

Chapter Six
    Catholicism in the Modern World   125

Selected Bibliography   149

Notes   157

Index   165

Preface

I first met Thomas Merton when, as a student in Louisville's Southern Baptist Theological Seminary, my class in church history visited Gethsemani Abbey near Bardstown to study monasticism first hand. We were honored that day with a lecture by the abbey's most famous monk, Father Louis, known in popular religion and American literature as Thomas Merton. My friends and I were intrigued by his lively personality, his enthusiastic interest in wide-ranging topics, his infectious humor, and his ability to field our most difficult questions, proving in the process his dedication to reading and inquiry. Although during the next few years I enjoyed reading his autobiography, *The Seven Storey Mountain*, his other books, products of his early mysticism, were for the most part singularly unappealing to one who thought of himself as a worldly man. However, later in the 1960s, his writings began to sound a note of social concern, and their refreshing thesis of spiritual, social, and religious union, while not really new to him, suddenly began to make sense to all of us who were laboring in man's world for society's improvement. The Protestant theologians that I had read had taught me to recognize the brokenness of man's society, and the unfolding events of the 1960s proved the truth of their theory. Merton's call for spiritual and social union, a poetic and sometimes unimplemented solution to alienation and division, was a valid and authentic, if at times limited, response to the contemporary chaos. A cloistered monk, in spite of or perhaps because of his distance from world events, could not only see the questions being raised by the 1960s but could strain his faith for answers to them.

When my doctoral program in the humanities at Florida State University required a subject for research, I chose Thomas Merton, not knowing precisely what I would find but convinced that the man and his long shelf of books were worth investigating. I corresponded with Merton, visited him at Gethsemani, and in 1968 completed a dissertation entitled "Thomas Merton: The Spiritual and Social Philosophy of Union," the first of a long series of theses and dissertations on Merton now completed or in process. I began teaching at Western Kentucky University in Bowling Green, ninety miles from Merton at Gethsemani, in 1968, anticipating the opportunity to study Merton's thought as it developed further. Then with Christmas 1968 came the news of his accidental and tragic death in Bangkok.

This book is a labor of obligation and love in behalf of one who personally and professionally meant so much to me at a time of great change in my own philosophy of life. While I could wish it were presently uncalled for and that Thomas Merton were still alive and well and writing his yearly reams of poetry and social criticism, the past cannot be changed, and I can only hope that this book will bring together in an adequate fashion the social outlook of this man who, while primarily a monk, became toward the end of his life a man of the world. If at times the reader feels that I am treating Merton too easily, it is because I am convinced that, in spite of some rather glaring errors in judgment, his basic thesis and consequent outlook are accurate and that to clarify them for further study and teaching is my primary purpose and task. I must admit that in one sense, although I am still a Protestant and have no intention of becoming a monk, I am one of Thomas Merton's converts.

While writing the dissertation and then the book I visited Gethsemani Abbey ten times, twice for personal interviews with Merton and eight times to do research in the abbey's Thomas Merton Room since his death. During my first visit with him we discussed through a cold lenten afternoon in 1968 my major theses, evaluations, and conclusions, and the answers that he gave me, combined with the experience of talking intimately with the man himself, helped correct a number of errors. In July 1968 Merton wrote to me acknowledging receipt of a copy of the dissertation, saying that he thought it was an accurate and fair appraisal of his thought, offering suggestions for improving it, and inviting my wife and me to visit him, which we did on September 4, 1968, a week before he left for the Orient. He told me then that he was glad a Protestant was his first interpreter, since he usually received either unthinking praise or condemnation from Catholics.

Since his death I have made a number of trips to the Thomas Merton Collection at Bellarmine College in Louisville and to the Thomas Merton Room at Gethsemani, finding both to be excellent if as yet not completely organized sources for Merton research. The Thomas Merton Collection at Bellarmine features copies of his published and unpublished manuscripts as well as his taped lectures, drawings, photographs, and personal memorabilia from his youth and monastic career. The room at Gethsemani, tucked away in a far corner of the enclosed library and more limited in sources, nevertheless includes such interesting items as copies of Merton's works in their typewritten form, sometimes with his own corrections penciled in, Merton's books in foreign translations, some books from his personal library, notes which he made on various subjects, his father's confirmation Bible, and a stole which Pope John XXIII wore in his coronation and sent to Merton as a personal gift. There also I found the copy of my dissertation which Merton had corrected; these corrections have been included in this book. Merton's unpublished diaries and untold numbers of other unpublished manuscripts are as yet unavailable to the general public or even Merton scholars; they are now being researched by John Howard Griffin, who has been designated Merton's official biographer by the Merton Legacy Trust Committee. It is hoped that they will be released for study after the biography is published in 1972. Those who wish to do research on Thomas Merton may go either to Bellarmine College, where they can research freely as long as they sign an agreement drawn up by the Legacy Trust Committee concerning the use of unpublished manuscripts, or to Gethsemani Abbey, where the monks are most helpful.

To mention all the people who have contributed directly to this work would require a chapter in itself. However, I would especially like to thank the Committee for Faculty Research at Western Kentucky University which provided the funds to continue my research and revision. Also responsible for the completion of this work are Dr. Glen Hinson of The Southern Baptist Theological Seminary, who helped me cut through some of the sanctified red tape which at first prevented me from corresponding with Thomas Merton; Dr. Charles Wellborn, who directed the doctoral dissertation at Florida State University; Jill Baker, my wife and personal confidante, whose encouragement forced me to press on with my study even in moments of self-doubt; and the monks of Gethsemani, particularly Brothers Patrick and Benedict, who have sent me manuscripts and helped me find materials in the Thomas Merton Room and in general made me feel at home when visiting the abbey.

Chapter One

The Pilgrim's Progress

Thomas Merton was born on January 31, 1915, in Prades, a French village lying in the Pyrenees Mountains near the Spanish border. His parents, both artists, had met in Paris and had come to the south of France to paint. His father was Owen Merton, a New Zealander of Welsh extraction; his mother, Ruth Jenkins, was the daughter of a successful publisher on Long Island. Merton always attributed his own adult personality to his parents who were, he said, captives in the world but not captives of it. In his autobiography he wrote: "I inherited from my father his way of looking at things and some of his integrity and from my mother some of her dissatisfaction with the mess the world is in, and some of her versatility. From both I got capacities for work and vision and enjoyment and expression that ought to have made me some kind of a King, if the standards the world lives by were the real ones."[1]

The young Thomas was properly baptized, his father being a devoted if sometimes negligent Anglican, but he was not taken to church during his early childhood because his mother openly despised formal religion, attending only Quaker services occasionally. She believed that church traditions would corrupt her son, and although he sometimes asked to be taken to that mysterious place where the bells were ringing on Sunday morning, she consistently refused his pleas. He later speculated that had his mother lived he would doubtless have become a nice skeptic: an author, editor, or professor in a small, progressive liberal arts college.[2]

As the Great War in Europe intensified, Owen Merton fled with his wife and son to America where he became a gardener in Flushing, Long Island, five miles from his father-in-law's home in Douglaston. There in 1918 Thomas's only brother, John Paul, was born. John Paul was to be the last child born to the Merton family, for Mrs. Merton, shortly thereafter, was hospitalized with inoperable cancer. As soon as his wife entered the hospital, Owen Merton moved with his two sons to Douglaston and took a job as organist in the local Episcopal church, at the same time continuing to paint and do gardening as well as to play the piano at the town movie house. For the first time young Thomas attended church regularly with his father. He would later remember coming out of the services each Sunday with little more than the feeling that he had done something that needed doing, but he always felt grateful for this bit of religion that he received during his mother's illness. His only real religious training during this time consisted of learning the Lord's Prayer from his grandmother Merton, who had come to America from New Zealand for a visit.

With his mother's death Thomas's life began to break up, and he was not to know again a completely settled and secure existence until he became a monk. His father, now free to travel and devote all his time to painting, first took Thomas with him to Bermuda, painted there for several months, returned to New York where he had a successful exhibit, and then left Thomas with his grandparents while he went to paint in France.

During these next few months spent with his American grandparents, Thomas got part of his education from the flickering, yellow-lighted movies that were still being made and shown on Long Island and from the cheap reprints of popular novels, methodically produced by his grandfather's publishing firm. His religious training in Douglaston, he said, was typical of the semitolerant religious theology of the upper-middle class at that time. The general attitude was that all religions were "more or less praiseworthy on purely natural or social grounds"—all religions, that is, except Roman Catholicism. The Roman Catholic Church was thought to be synonymous with Tammany Hall, and Tammany Hall was in turn thought to be synonymous with all sorts of corruption. Merton later explained that the vague and evil thing called Catholicism lived in the dark corners of his mind along with other spooks like death, and he remembered, "I did not know precisely what the word meant. It only conveyed a kind of cold and unpleasant feeling."[3]

Owen Merton, having achieved a measure of fame in a successful London exhibit, returned to New York in 1925 and announced that he would take Thomas with him to Europe where he would eventually attend school in England. The artist and his son arrived in Paris in August 1925 and set out immediately for the south of France where they settled in Saint Antonin, an ancient city originally established by the Romans, and built a house with a large studio below and two bedrooms above. For several months the two of them lived together in this house; from there they took long walks through the hills and lived the free life of independent men. While his father painted, Thomas would wander through a countryside so steeped in Catholic history that he seemed to enter into the Sacraments just by breathing the air; he came to love the cathedral in Saint Antonin and the ruins of the old abbey, and he would say much later that his contemplative life, like his physical life, began in the south of France.[4]

After several months of attending a lycée in nearby Mountauban, Thomas was taken by his father to England and enrolled in the Ripley Court School, where he studied until he was fourteen years of age. During these four years he went through what he called his first religious phase, becoming a devout Anglican, attending church regularly, and praying before meals and bed. Fifteen years later, having become a Catholic monk, he would remember this period with mixed emotions: "Prayer is attractive enough when it is considered in a context of good food, and sunny joyous country churches, and the green English countryside. And, as a matter of fact, the Church of England means all this. It is a class religion, the cult of a special society and group, not even of a whole nation, but of the ruling minority in a nation."[5]

In the autumn of 1929 he was admitted to the Oakham school, an English public school. During his first year at Oakham his father died of a malignant brain tumor, leaving him an orphan, but his American grandfather, fearing bankruptcy in those years of the great depression, gave him an insurance policy sufficient to pay all his expenses and make him financially independent for the next few years. And so he was set free to do as he pleased with neither parental nor financial hindrances, an enviable situation for a boy of seventeen, but the years of freedom that lay ahead proved to be exceedingly unhappy ones.

One reason for his unhappiness was his loss of faith, for the years at Oakham gradually made him despise the Church of England, which was the only kind of religion that he knew. He came to hate the Anglican church because of its embarrassing ties with and support of the British aristocracy, and he found especially distasteful the theology that grew out of this relationship. For example, he remembered that in what he called characteristic Anglican fashion the chaplain at Oakham interpreted the word *charity* in 1 Corinthians 13 as "gentlemanliness." Every time the apostle Paul said *charity* the chaplain said *gentlemanliness,* or at least gave it that definition. Thus he would conclude that even if a young Englishman should speak with the tongue of angels and were not a gentleman he would be as sounding brass and a tinkling cymbal. Merton, already showing signs of his later humor, recalled, "I will not accuse him of finishing the chapter with 'Now there remain faith, hope, and gentlemanliness, and the greatest of these is gentlemanliness . . .' although it was the logical term of his reasoning."[6]

Merton filled the vacuum caused by his loss of faith with the study of literature and languages, being particularly attracted by the works of James Joyce, D. H. Lawrence, T. S. Eliot, Ernest Hemingway, and Evelyn Waugh. But the two writers who most influenced his early thinking and literary style were William Blake and Gerard Manley Hopkins. He had read Blake as a child, but he now rediscovered him in all his symbolic majesty. He was most impressed by Blake's antipathy toward false piety and religiosity, the scandals of the Anglican faith which Merton was in the process of condemning, and by Blake's admiration for the man who genuinely loves God. He discovered Hopkins while in a hospital bed. During his last year at Oakham he visited Germany to make the traditional walk down the Rhine but was soon hospitalized with blood poisoning; while convalescing he was given a book of Hopkins's poetry and soon became a loyal devotee of this great Catholic writer to whom he has been compared in recent years.

In January 1933 Merton passed his entrance examinations and was accepted as a student at Cambridge University. Since he would not enter Cambridge until the autumn term he decided to tour Italy during the spring and summer and to spend most of his time in Rome. This trip proved to be a decisive experience, although he did not recognize it as such at the time, for he experienced a kind of conversion both to a culture and to a religion, a conversion which he would at first dismiss as the foolishness of adolescence but one to which he would return after many years of wandering.

When he first arrived in Rome he spent most of his time visiting museums and searching through the ruins of the classical Roman age. But he was soon attracted to the churches, both old and new, and in this way discovered a completely different Rome—one that his schooling had not taught him—Christian Rome. Especially impressed by the Byzantine mosaics in the early churches, he began reading the Bible each night in order to understand the artistic representations in the churches that he visited by day. He also began praying in each of the churches, and after overcoming the initial embarrassment of praying in public, an embarrassment which most Protestants but few Catholics understand, he found this practice most rewarding.

One night in his hotel room, after a day of prayer and study, he seemed to feel the presence of his father with him and responded to this mystical experience by praying. After a few minutes the emotion passed, but he kept the memory of his father in his heart and continued to pray whenever he had the opportunity. His visits to the Roman churches thereafter became even more significant to him, and following a visit to the Trappist monastery Tré Fontane he confided to an acquaintance that he would someday like to become a monk like those he had just seen.[7]

He sailed from Rome that summer to visit his family on Long Island. While in America he visited several types of churches, intent upon discovering a spiritual home in which to continue the religious quest begun in Rome, but in each instance he was disappointed. He concluded that the Episcopal priest of the church where his father had been organist had abandoned Christian theology for discussions of literature and politics, and although he expressed admiration for the Quaker silence he concluded that in their testimonial services they simply substituted lay inanities for clerical ones. Despite his experiences in the churches of Rome, he apparently did not seriously consider becoming a Catholic, still thinking of the Catholic church in America as somehow the ally of Tammany Hall and failing to make the connection between the churches of Rome and the Roman Catholic Church.[8]

By the time he returned to England and entered Cambridge his religious zeal had diminished and his "conversion" was forgotten. Although he had planned to pursue a strenuous course of studies to prepare himself for British diplomatic service, he soon became dissipated and unhappy and came to hate Cambridge. He later said that the one valuable thing he received from his single year at that British university was a thorough acquaintance with Dante, whom he always thereafter considered the greatest of all Catholic poets. He was therefore pleased when, at the end of his first year at Cambridge and after a scandal led his British guardian to refuse further responsibility for him, his grandfather asked him to give up his plans for a career in the diplomatic corps and come to live in New York. He gladly left England forever in November 1934 and would ever after demonstrate a decidedly anti-British bias in his writings.

Upon arriving in New York with no definite plans or goal in life, his first project was to find himself. During his first few months in New York he seemed to be searching frantically for his place in a society which was new to him, and he seemed determined to find a philosophy of life, no matter what it might be. He first became an admirer of communism, seeing every available Russian movie and expressing deep admiration for the progress which Russia had made under communism. Despite the scenes of the Kremlin and Red Square, which he later admitted contained the world's ugliest buildings, he hungrily swallowed the party line presented by these movies and loyally believed that Russia, where artists were said to be free from the dictates of bourgeois tastes, was truly the home of the arts. He came to believe that the intolerable conditions of the modern world were the products of materialistic capitalism and that the world could be cleansed only by capitalism's demise. Communism was an appealing philosophy to an unhappy young man like Merton, for it permitted him to blame his failures and unhappiness on society and reject all personal responsibility for them.[9]

Upon entering Columbia University in January 1935, Merton came into contact with a number of Communists, the first he had ever met. He found that the Columbia Communists were primarily undergraduates, not faculty members as the Hearst papers were claiming, and that their voice was much louder than their size merited because they controlled the school paper, *The Specta-*

tor. But he joined the Young Communist League, perhaps because of its unpopularity, taking the party name Frank Swift. He even attended a Communist outing at the Park Avenue apartment of a member whose parents were away for the weekend, but the irony of this situation and the usual dullness of the meetings combined to drive him out of active membership after about three months.

He then joined the National Students League, the campus Socialist organization, and one of his first tasks was to picket the Casa Italiana with a sign condemning Italy's actions in Ethiopia. He said later that even at the time he realized the futility of this demonstration but considered it a public confession of faith, a protest against all war. In fact, he had become a Socialist primarily because the Socialists were emphasizing pacifism that year, and he was a pacifist. Along with several hundred other students he attended a Socialist rally on campus and signed the Oxford Pledge, promising that he would never participate in any war, but his faith in socialism was somewhat shaken the following year when the leaders of that rally went to Spain to fight with the Communists against the fascist general Francisco Franco.

During these early years at Columbia it was only his cynicism that saved Merton from becoming, as Eric Hoffer would say, a true believer in communism or socialism. He was desperately searching for a faith, a philosophy of life, a purpose, but each of the options that he examined had a fatal flaw which Merton's perceptive mind quickly brought to light. He was a wary searcher after meaning in life, a young man who was looking for something to believe in but who would look long and hard before making a commitment.

Despite his failure to find a faith and his disillusionment with communism and socialism, Merton's early years at Columbia were a time of great personal growth. Years after graduation, when he could reflect upon the various influences that had molded his life, he would place Columbia at the top of the list. In a manuscript explaining his philosophy of education, he said that Columbia had given him the most precious gift any man could receive: a good education. He believed that the purpose of education is to help the student "define himself authentically and spontaneously in relation to his world" and that a university's primary task is to help its students discover themselves. The university, he said, should help the student save his soul from the "hell of meaninglessness, of obsession, of complex artifice, of systematic lying, of criminal evasions and neglects, of self-destructive futilities," and Columbia had done this for him. Most of all Columbia had taught him the value of unsuccess. Instead of adapting him to the downtown New York world, he said, Columbia lobbed him "half conscious" into Greenwich Village where he occasionally came to his senses and continued to learn. Columbia also strongly influenced the development of Thomas Merton the contemplative:

> The thing I always liked best about Columbia was the sense that the University was, on the whole, glad to turn me loose in its library, its classrooms, and among its distinguished faculty, and let me make what I liked out of it all. I did. And I ended up by being turned on like a pin ball machine by Blake, Thomas Aquinas, Augustine, Eckhart, Coomaraswamy, Traherne, Hopkins, Maritain, and the sacraments of the Catholic Church. After which I came to the monastery in which (this is public knowledge) I have continued to be the same kind of maverick and have in fact ended as a hermit who is also fully identified with the peace movement, with Zen, with a group of Latin American hippie poets, etc. etc.[10]

Columbia apparently helped to create the personality that would one day be the world's most outspoken monk since Martin Luther and the most conspicuous recluse since Simeon Stylites.

During his undergraduate years at Columbia he spent most of his free time at his grandparents' home in Douglaston. Will Lissner, a writer who lived near Douglaston in the 1930s and 1940s, described the town as a bayside community of spacious but unpretentious houses, with an abundance of boats, tennis courts, and golf courses. Merton was long remembered by the local residents as a powerful swimmer and a gregarious but somewhat peculiar young man who enjoyed taking long walks in the dead of winter.[11]

On campus Merton was active in literary circles, writing for every school publication, especially *The Spectator,* the *Review,* and *Jester,* and editing the 1937 edition of the year book, *The Columbian.* He seemed to be drifting toward a career in journalism. His reward for the time and energy spent on campus publications came when his graduating class, by a margin of twelve votes, named him the best writer of the year. Years later he discussed the minor scandal that marred this election. Most of the graduating class believed that the boy chosen "most likely to succeed" had made a deal with the one chosen "best dressed" and that together they had doctored the vote to assure their victories. Merton was not accused of being involved in any plots, but it was common knowledge that his fraternity brothers, voting as a bloc, had secured his election in a close race.

He would later see his undergraduate years at Columbia as formative and full of excitement, but at the time they were characterized by unhappiness and loneliness. He was a long time in finding anything to believe in and found most of his activities unsatisfying. Despite his intellectual bent, he led a mildly wicked and an extremely strenuous social life, often staying out all night in the city and arriving home at dawn feeling deeply embarrassed at riding in the same coach with the healthy and purposeful working-men on their way to the factories. During his last year in under-graduate school his grandfather and soon thereafter his grand-mother died, leaving him alone except for his brother, and he suffered some type of physical or nervous breakdown just before he was to graduate. This illness caused him to abandon his earlier ambition to be a journalist, for it made him fear that he would always suffer from ill health, and he decided instead to enter Columbia's graduate program in English and prepare for a career as a teacher. He later recalled that this was his first step away from money and fame and toward contemplation, since he had then decided to live the rest of his life in the relative peace of a college campus, reading and writing books.[12]

A number of men—teachers, writers, and fellow students—affected Merton's personal development during his undergraduate years at Columbia. One of the most important was Mark Van Doren, his teacher, whom Merton credited with leading him to his understanding of literature. He recalled that what Van Doren taught was actually literature, not biography, speculation, theory, or sociology about literature. He said: "It was a very good thing for me that I ran into someone like Mark Van Doren at that particular time, because in my new reverence for Communism, I was in danger of docilely accepting any kind of stupidity, provided I thought it was something that paved the way to the Elysian fields of classless society."[13]

Another man who helped him define himself was a Hindu monk from India, Bramachari. Bramachari had been sent by his superior to represent his monastery at the Chicago World's Fair in 1936. Without money or passport he had arrived in America too late for the fair but thereafter managed to earn a doctorate from the University of Chicago. He remained for several years in the United States, speaking to college groups and discussing religion with anyone who wanted to talk. In conversations with Merton at Columbia, Bramachari maintained that Christianity and the West as a whole needed a revival of asceticism and suggested that he read some of the better Western books, such as Augustine's *City of God* and Thomas à Kempis's *Imitation of Christ*. Merton evidently took his advice, for these books not only became his constant companions but eventually helped lead him to his decision to become a monk.

Etienne Gilson, a Roman Catholic philosopher, also influenced Merton's intellectual and religious development through his writings on Christian theology. During his senior year Merton bought Gilson's *Spirit of Medieval Philosophy,* not realizing that it was a "Catholic" book. When he opened it and saw the traditional "Nihil Obstat . . . Imprimatur" he was disgusted, for no matter how much he admired Catholic culture he still distrusted the Roman Catholic Church and especially its censorship. However, since he was taking a course in medieval French literature he read the book as background material and was so impressed by its contents that he came to think of Gilson as a saint. He was particularly impressed by Gilson's discussion of aseity, the statement that God is Being per se, that he has no cause; this concept seemed to free God from all the inadequate but popular representations which Merton had learned as a child.

It was in 1938, when he wrote his master's thesis at Columbia, that all the ideas and influences from his undergraduate years and earlier finally converged and led Merton to his religious conversion. In January of that year he completed the requirements for his baccalaureate in English and immediately entered upon a course of study leading to the master's degree in that same field. Not surprisingly, he chose to write his thesis on "Nature and Art in William Blake." Since childhood he had been interested in Blake and had often discussed Blake's writings and art with his father. Now the deeper inquiry into Blake's thought required by his research and writing brought about a change in the whole direction of his life. He sought to synthesize Blake's romanticism with Jacques Maritain's mysticism as represented in *Art and Scholasticism,* and most influential upon his conclusions was his own father's belief that the artistic and religious experiences are virtually identical. By the time the thesis was completed Merton had decided that the only life for him was in religion, a life filled with the presence of God.[14] Blake's importance to him can be seen in the conclusion of "Journal of My Escape from the Nazis," a novel written a year later, when Merton said: "I think suddenly of Blake, filling paper with words, so that the words flew about the room for the angels to read, and after that, what if the paper was lost or destroyed? That is the only reason for wanting to write, Blake's reason."[15]

Merton's first year of graduate study ended with his firm commitment to the Catholic faith. He began attending group discussions led by several Columbia students who were interested in the church, and after taking a course in scholastic philosophy under Professor Daniel Walsh he began attending mass regularly. Finding in the church both the purpose and the philosophy of life that he had been seeking for such a long time, he was baptized a Roman Catholic in November 1938.

Early the next year he received his master's degree and began working toward his doctorate, planning to write his dissertation on Gerard Manley Hopkins. The coming war in Europe occupied much of his thought in those days, and feeling partly responsible for all the evil troubling the world, he turned to his new faith for support, attending mass regularly and praying for peace. He feared that another war would destroy the Europe that he loved, and out of his pessimism came the poem "Fable for a War" which won the Marian Griswald van Rensselaer Annual Poetry Prize in 1939. Its prophetic words are still appropriate today.

> Europe is a feast
> For every bloody beast;
> Jackals will grow fat
> On the bones after that,
> But in the end of all
> None but the crows can sing the funeral.[16]

Merton's still-fresh religious conversion, his even more recent baptism into the church, and his failure to see any positive hope for the strife-torn world led him in 1939 to make what would prove to be the most important decision of his life. After a sleepless night he told some of his friends that he intended to become a priest and maybe even enter a monastery. All that day he thought about this abrupt decision, and in the evening he entered a church and promised God that he would indeed be a monk. He decided to choose an order that would detach him from the world and unite him with God, "not a Rule made to fit me to fight for God in the world." He particularly wanted solitude to expand himself by baring his soul to God. His teacher and friend Daniel Walsh suggested that he become a Trappist and even offered to help him make a retreat to the Trappist monastery in Kentucky, but when Merton learned that the Trappists were reformed Cistercians and that they observed a strict rule of silence, he decided against them, choosing rather to apply for membership in the Order of Saint Francis. He was accepted and planned to enter their training program in August 1940, with the eventual goal of teaching English literature in a Franciscan college, not as ideally sacrificial a career as he had expected but one perhaps better suited to his personality.

In the spring of 1940 Merton decided to visit a number of Catholic shrines in Cuba as a kind of religious vacation before becoming a Franciscan. His journal is filled with praise for the architecture and the mysticism of Latin American Catholicism, but while the Cuban shrines increased his devotion to Jesus Christ they did not still a vague but growing doubt about his monastic vocation. Upon returning to New York he explained this puzzling doubt to his Franciscan adviser, and after a few days of nervous anticipation he was told that his admission to the order had been canceled. Deeply embarrassed by this rejection, he refused to give up his commitment to the monastic ideal, and he bought a breviary, determining to live as a monk in the world by keeping all the rules and attending mass every day. In order to remain in close contact with the Franciscans he accepted a teaching position at Saint Bonaventure's College near Olean, New York, and began teaching English there in September 1940. He enjoyed teaching the classes made up primarily of theology students and football players, and he had time to write some poetry (a skill which he said he developed only after his baptism) and to think through his philosophy of life, but he came to realize in the process of teaching and writing that his deepest desire was still for the monastic vocation.[17]

In November 1940 he registered for the draft, and he later recalled how he felt at that time: "Indeed, perhaps now that I had just begun to taste my security, it would be taken away again, and

I would be cast back into the midst of violence and uncertainty and blasphemy and the play of anger and hatred and all passion, worse than ever before. It would be the wages of my own twenty-five years: this war was what I had earned for myself and the world. I could hardly complain that I was being drawn into it."[18] He began to think through his attitude toward participation in the war, especially since he would have to decide whether to register as a conscientious objector. In his college days he had made a purely emotional objection to war; now he felt it his duty to take a more enlightened and reasonable stand. In order to be just, the new Catholic and older pacifist decided, the war would have to be defensive, and since the average person could not know whether it was or not, he would simply have to trust the leadership in Washington. But he decided to register as a noncombatant objector, agreeing to serve in the medical corps as long as he did not have to drop bombs or fire a gun. He felt that he could do more good by aiding his fellowmen in places of danger than by turning his back on the war altogether. Ironically, after agonizing over the moral dilemma of serving in the army and after coming to a satisfactory conclusion concerning his own position and status, he failed his induction physical examination because he had too few teeth.

Once more free to plan for the future, Merton began to think again of the Trappists, that order which he had so admired in Italy but had tried to avoid since becoming a Catholic. To satisfy his curiosity about them, he attended the Easter retreat in 1941 at Our Lady of Gethsemani Abbey near Bardstown, Kentucky, the abbey suggested by Daniel Walsh. This pilgrimage proved to be decisive for his future, for his imagination was so stirred by the dedicated monks, living in silent devotion to God, that he immediately wanted to join their order. He wrote in his journal that week: "This is the center of America. I had wondered what was holding the country together, what was keeping the universe from cracking in pieces and falling apart. It is places like this monastery —not only this one: there must be others. This is the only real city in America—and it is by itself, in the wilderness. It is an axle around which the whole country blindly turns."[19]

When he entered the monastery and felt the great doors close behind him, shutting out the world, he felt the "deep, deep silence of the night, and of peace, and of holiness enfold me like love, like safety." Later, in his autobiography, he would describe his first impression of Gethsemani: "This is the center of all the vitality that is in America. This is the cause and reason why the nation is holding together. These men, hidden in the anonymity of their choir and their white cowls, are doing for their land what no army, no congress, no president could even do as such: they are winning for it the grace and the protection and the friendship of God."[20] And when, at the end of the retreat, he returned to Louisville to catch the train for New York, he discovered that everything in the world looked insipid and insane to him; he felt that he had lived for a moment in a world of true order and had left it. Then one night, soon after his return to Saint Bonaventure's, he opened his Bible and put his finger on a verse at random, and when he read the verse he was convinced that God was speaking to him, for the verse contained God's words to Zachariah: Thou shalt be silent.

But just as he was becoming convinced that he should be a Trappist, Merton was confronted with another vocational choice. During the summer term at Saint Bonaventure's one of the guest lecturers was Baroness Catherine de Huech Doherty, a lady of the Russian nobility who had escaped the October Revolution and settled in New York. After working as a laundress for a time, she had established a Catholic mission in Harlem, and in her lecture she explained that she needed Catholic volunteers to work among the Negroes of New York City. She specifically asked Merton to work with her and even promised him his mornings free from work so that he could write. After visiting Friendship House for a weekend, he agreed to come and work there in January, when the fall term ended at Saint Bonaventure's. In *The Seven Storey Mountain* he described his decision this way: "At least I could go to Harlem, and join these people in their tenement, and live on what God gave us to eat from day to day, and share my life with the sick and the starving and the dying and those who had never had anything and never would have anything, the outcasts of the earth, a race despised. If that was where I belonged, God would let me know soon enough and definitely enough."[21]

These words, however, were written several years after he actually faced the decision. His feelings at the time were somewhat different, as revealed by his journal. At the time he felt that to go to Harlem would be a pale imitation of what had now become his greatest desire: the Trappist monastic life. In the journal that would much later be published under the title *The Secular Journal of*

Thomas Merton, he wrote: "Going to live in Harlem does not seem to me to be anything special. It is a good and reasonable way to follow Christ. But going to the Trappists is exciting, its fills me with awe and with desire, I return to the idea again and again. 'Give up *everything,* give up everything.' "[22] This early journal reveals that he was already a monk at heart, and Paul Elmen, who reviewed the journal when it was published in 1959, was right when he commented: "If one could have studied this young man in 1941, emerging from the subway into the full glare of Morningside Heights, he would have seen crepe-soled shoes worn like sandals, a belt which had begun to suggest a cincture, and eyes already in custody."[23]

Merton's vague dissatisfaction with his plan to work in Harlem and his growing desire to be a Trappist led him to dedicate himself more fervently to prayer; the saint to whom he began praying was Saint Therese of Lisieux, known to her devotees as the Little Flower. One night at Saint Bonaventure's, being filled with a profound desire to become a Trappist, he went out into the woods near the campus and asked Saint Therese to show him a sign which would tell him what to do. While praying, he said, he suddenly heard the bells of Gethsemani Abbey as though they were calling him home from just beyond the nearest hill. A moment passed before he fully realized that the bells were only in his imagination, but he later calculated that at that very moment the bells at Gethsemani had indeed been ringing the *Salve Regina.*

Then and there he decided to attend the Christmas retreat at Gethsemani and to apply for admission as a novice at that time, but within a week he received a summons from his draft board. The standards for induction had been lowered because of the Japanese attack on Pearl Harbor, and his teeth would no longer hold up his induction. He wrote to the draft board, telling them of his desire to be a monk, and the board permitted him a delay of one month, long enough to be accepted or rejected by the Trappists. The other English teachers at Saint Bonaventure's divided his teaching load for the remainder of the term, and he caught a train for Kentucky, not knowing at the time whether he would be accepted or not. But he was warmly welcomed into the abbey on December 10, 1941, and given the name Brother Louis.[24] By accepting Thomas Merton into their community, the Trappists received a mixed blessing. He proved to be a Trojan horse of surprises, some good and some bad. He would, through his writings, bring both spiritual devotion and worldly fame to the tiny island of peace, attracting many new volunteers but turning the pitiless light of public scrutiny upon the abbey.

And so the brilliant young world traveler became a monk, sworn to silence and solitude. In order to understand this somewhat puzzling decision, one must first understand Merton the man. He was a gregarious person who enjoyed the company of other men yet felt a vital need for communication with God, and the monastery provided a community life with men who shared this quest. Life in the world gave him an acquaintance with thousands of people but no true community, and its noise and activity blocked effective contemplation. Far from abandoning society when he entered the monastery, he was actually seeking a new and better society. Although he could talk very little with his fellow monks because of the rule of silence, he soon learned the sign language with which the monks communicated, and in the monastery, among the silent, devoted brothers he found community: human companionship coupled with divine solitude. Through the years, as he began to teach the novices, he came to know his community even better, and his later social writings indicate the extent that the community influenced his developing thought.

There was also his disillusionment with the world. He had tasted all the pleasures of American and European society, yet he had found no meaning either in the world or in his role as a citizen of the world. He had, however, found a certain amount of satisfaction and meaning in the church and wanted more of the same. Being accepted into the monastery, then, was essentially a second baptism, an entrance into a deeper communion, a deeper involvement with reality. His decision to go to Gethsemani was a retreat from a meaningless existence to one which he believed would have meaning now and in eternity.

There was also his desire to become a saint, a desire which he insisted he shared with all good Catholics but which was unusually apparent in his own actions. His initial step in applying to the Franciscan order, his prayers to Saint Therese, and his eventual decision to enter Gethsemani all demonstrate the importance of this factor in his actions. His desire to stop writing once he became a monk, his research into the lives of the saints, and his retirement to a hermitage also demonstrate this ambition. Because a man who lives in a monastery has more spiritual discipline and greater religious motivation, he has a better chance than the average man to become a saint, and Merton wanted this opportunity.

During the last year of his life Merton discussed his reasons for becoming a monk. He placed the most emphasis upon the absolute nature of the monastic vocation, saying that the monastery offered him a definiteness that he could find nowhere else. The volunteer work in Harlem was a temporary vocation, he explained, one that was as subject to change as college teaching had been, and he was looking for a permanent vocation. To become a monk would be to commit oneself to a way of life that was final.

Merton sought a true community of men who were involved in the search for reality, who had given up the world in order to find meaning in life, and who were in the process of becoming saints. He believed that he had found such a place at Gethsemani, and being an individual who cared little for the established customs of man's society he became a monk, perhaps not realizing at the time the nature or extent of his new subordination to monastic customs. He would be as much a rebel in the monastery as he had been outside it.

Merton assumed that by entering a Trappist monastery he was disengaging himself from the world, for the Trappists have traditionally opposed intellectual and social endeavors, devoting most of their time and energy to worship and physical labor in the fields. However, the Trappist community at Gethsemani faced new challenges in the 1940s. Large numbers of laymen and priests began coming to every retreat held at the monastery, scores of new monastic volunteers were entering the gates every year, and some of these new Trappists, being better educated than their predecessors, were beginning to write for publication. Merton's educational and linguistic background and his tendency to delicate health led his superiors, his abbot Dom Frederic Dunne and his teacher Dom Robert, to decide that his labor would be intellectual: translating, writing poetry, researching the lives of saints, writing books, and teaching novices. Far from retreating into obscurity, he suddenly found himself writing more and being read and heard by more people than ever before.

He was for several years deeply disturbed by the fact that he spent so much of his time writing; he had originally entered Gethsemani to save his soul and become a saint, he argued, but he found himself being told to write as much as he prayed. Brother Louis came to think of Thomas Merton as the man who followed him into the cloister and dogged his steps continually, refusing to die at the monastery door as his role in the drama demanded. Brother Louis described Thomas Merton this way:

> He is a business man. He is full of ideas. He breathes notions and new schemes. He generates books in the silence that ought to be sweet with the infinitely productive darkness of contemplation.
> And the worst of it is, he has my superiors on his side. They won't kick him out. I can't get rid of him.
> Maybe in the end he will kill me, he will drink my blood.
> Nobody seems to understand that one of us has got to die.[25]

The journal which Merton kept between 1946 and 1952 is called *The Sign of Jonas,* and he explained in the introduction that during those years he felt that, like Jonas, he was traveling toward his destiny "in the belly of a paradox," or in a way at odds with his own desires. The Trappist vow of stability, the vow to stay in one place, intended to set a monk free from the worry of having to move, had proved to be for him the belly of the whale. He had come to the monastery to find perfect solitude, but he had not found it because of his writing, and for a time he seriously considered leaving Gethsemani to join the more rigidly disciplined Carthusian order. Later he concluded that God knew all along how much solitude he needed and gave him the proper orders through his superiors, but at the time he had to fight the temptation of Jonas, the temptation to run the other way.[26]

He admitted to his confessor in the late 1940s that for some time he had secretly longed to leave his writing behind him and become a Carthusian, that he had remained in Gethsemani only because Europe was at war and there were no Charterhouses in America, and that now that the war was over he was once again tempted to leave Gethsemani, not because the life was too strict but indeed because it was not strict enough. But his confessor convinced him that his desire to become a Carthusian was full of self-love and that only a mighty upheaval in his life would justify his leaving Gethsemani. Next he asked Dom Frederic for permission to spend more time in meditation and less time writing, but he refused, and when Merton described this interview sadly in his journal he concluded with a sigh, "So that is that." But one month later an entry shows that he had justified the decision to himself and had reconciled himself to it. He had settled down to being a writer and had solved his problem by learning to pray and write simultaneously. He explained: "I can see that it is much better for me to go on trying to learn to write under the strange conditions imposed by Cistercian life. I can become a saint by writing well, for the glory of God, denying myself, judging myself, and mortifying my haste to get into print. Writing is a moral matter, and my typewriter is an essential factor in my asceticism."[27]

News from China also contributed to his decision to remain in the Cistercian order. He learned that with their "usual Communist tactics" the Chinese Reds had convinced the peasants that a group of Cistercian monks were the tools of capitalism and had led them to burn the monastery, convict the monks, and cart them all over China like animals in a circus. Somehow the suffering and courage of these Cistercians convinced Merton of the value of his order, and he realized the futility of daydreaming about becoming a Carthusian. It was "as if the dead Chinese monks, in the naked seriousness of their martyrdom, had killed the roots of this spiritual self-indulgence in my soul. It is no longer permitted to me to waste, in such a dream, the precious hours of my monastic life."[28] And so in 1952 he titled his journal *The Sign of Jonas* because his gloomy years of riding in the whale's belly ended in a kind of resurrection to new life. Merton accepted himself and his role as a monastic writer, and the story of Jonas began to make sense to him. The sign of Jonas was finally seen symbolically as the resurrection of Christ, believed by monks to be the power of the contemplative life. This justification was either a divine answer or an interesting bit of rationalization.

Merton's second abbot, Dom James Fox, has explained in a privately circulated manuscript that he required his intellectual monk to continue writing, as Dom Frederic before him had done, because he feared, given Merton's literary temperament, that the silent life with no outlet for artistic expression might lead to mental disturbance. Merton himself later admitted that writing was an essential part of his nature and that he would likely take a sheet of asbestos paper with him when he died so that he could write all the way through purgatory.

During the twenty-seven years of his monastic life Merton wrote, edited, and translated almost fifty books and almost three hundred articles, reviews, and poems for periodicals. He became a leading commentator on religion, society, and aesthetics, the most celebrated monk in the world. He distinguished himself as a writer of depth, skill, and purpose, a major voice in the American churches, both Catholic and Protestant. But in spite of his success as a writer he always longed for more privacy, for more time to contemplate. And so after reconciling himself to remaining at Gethsemani as a writer, he began to think about living as a hermit. As early as 1947 he asked his abbot whether any monks of the order had ever been permitted to become hermits. He was told of the one monk who had lived for a time in a hut out in the woods from the monastery and whose meditations were so interrupted by local people coming to him for spiritual counsel that he gladly returned to the monastery for some peace and quiet. Merton was thus discouraged from asking to live as a solitary, and he remained a part of the common community until 1965.

Thomas Merton was many complex, if not contradictory, things: an intellectual, a liberal, a converted Protestant-secularist, a child of the Enlightenment, a sophisticated poet, and a cosmopolitan traveler, but most of all he was a Catholic and a contemplative. A Catholic monastery made him what he was. He would probably have become a great writer had he never seen the inside of an abbey, for he possessed all the natural energy, insight, and creativity required to write profound and moving works of literature, but without the monastery he would have been a different writer. He would have known a quite different subject matter, and although he might have still become a famous Catholic writer, he would have been deprived of the surroundings which created the image, the atmosphere, the soul of Thomas Merton. The happy if paradoxical ending to *The Seven Storey Mountain* both made him famous and set the style for all his subsequent works. There was, indeed, an oriental paradox about his life and thought, the paradox of a monk speaking to the world, which gave it the quality that was uniquely Merton, and any other career would have robbed his work of that quality.

Without the security and strength of the church, and the monastery in particular, Merton might have been much more pessimistic. His works, although tempered by the traditional optimism of Catholic anthropology, were rather pessimistic, and had he not become a Catholic monk he would probably have continued to build upon his growing pessimism of the mid-1930s and might have moved further toward despair as the war subsided only to reveal the atomic bomb and the smoldering racial crisis. Outside the monastery his talents would probably have been invested in continually pointing out the absurdity of life, and he might have become a kind of American Camus, since his late interest in that French existentialist demonstrated their intellectual kinship.

His opinions about social issues would certainly have been modified by the give-and-take of debate outside the monastery. His criticism of the world and his suggestions for reform were obviously the work of a solitary genius, one whose ideals and conclusions were never tempered by the arguments of opponents. He admitted that his fellow monks were always angered or distressed when he raised controversial issues, even those of a spiritual nature, in his sermons or lectures to them; they preferred traditional, meditative approaches to problems, creating not the most stimulating environment for a social critic. Because Merton thought about social issues alone and was highly selective in his reading, his opinions were biased, although for the most part clearly on the side of truth; outside the absolute sanctity of the monastery he would have thought and written differently about social matters, but not necessarily better.

In the introduction to an anthology of his writings entitled *A Thomas Merton Reader,* Merton divided his monastic life into four distinct periods. A fifth period which he could not foresee at the time of this publication, the time of his hermitage and death, can now be added to these four. The first period was his novitiate, 1942–1944, the period of adjustment and of learning the ways of the monastic life. During these three years he wrote relatively little, but he later came to feel that the poetry which he wrote at that time was the best of his career. He published one book between 1942 and 1944, *Thirty Poems,* in which the reader may find examples of his early poetic style.

The second period began in 1944 when he said his First Vows and ended in 1949 when he was ordained a priest. In 1944 he suffered the first of two physical illnesses which caused him to decrease his work load for some time. The illness was first diagnosed as tuberculosis, and his superiors prescribed rest and meditation instead of his usual activities, but upon his recovery they assigned him to a study of philosophy and theology, to writing books and articles, and to translating other books and articles from French. His prose improved markedly during those years, and he produced such memorable volumes as *The Seven Storey Mountain, Seeds of Contemplation, Figures for an Apocalypse, A Man in the Divided Sea, The Waters of Siloe, The Tears of the Blind Lions,* and several lives of saints, which he later said he would just as soon forget.

The first of these books, *The Seven Storey Mountain,* became a best seller and made his name known throughout America and in parts of Europe. It has sold over a million copies since its publication in 1948 and has been translated into several languages. Merton even had to reject an offer from Hollywood to make it into a movie starring Don Ameche. Had he not signed a contract with the publishers for it before his order's censor read it, however, the book would never have been published. The censor at first rejected the manuscript, saying that it was thoroughly useless and would do much harm, but when he learned that the contract had already been signed he permitted it to pass saying that it should have been written fifty years later and by someone else.[29]

When Merton first conceived the idea of writing his autobiography early in 1944, he confessed it as a temptation, and while his confessor did not consider the desire to write his life's story a sin he did tease him for being so naive as to believe that anyone would be interested in reading the autobiography of a twenty-nine-year-old Trappist monk. But this book about a worldly young man who found peace and fulfillment in a Catholic monastery proved exceedingly attractive to an America searching for security following World War II. Catholics particularly liked it because it proved that their faith could attract and convert a young, sophisticated Protestant. It was published at the opportune moment, when Catholics and the American public as a whole were ready for it. Merton admitted later that he had always believed it would be a popular book—not particularly good but popular. He seemed to have understood the mood of America better than his confessor and better than many trained society-watchers outside the walls.

Soon after making Solemn Vows in 1947, Merton's writings began to be recognized by critics as having great value in the fields of religion and literature. In 1948 he received a citation from the

Literary Awards Committee of the Catholic Press Association of the United States for *Figures for an Apocalypse,* which was said to be "the most distinguished volume of verse published in English by a Catholic poet in 1948." In 1949 he won the annual Catholic Literary Award for *The Seven Storey Mountain,* presented by the Gallery of Living Catholic Authors. Thus began his climb to fame, a climb which he would have gladly traded for more time in worship and prayer, a fame which he did not want but richly deserved.

In 1951 he wrote in his journal that he considered *The Seven Storey Mountain* and *Thirty Poems* to be his only decent books and that he wished they were the only books he had ever published. By 1967 his self-criticism had increased, and he seemed to regret even the publication of *The Seven Storey Mountain.* He explained to a friend that he had left that book behind him many years ago and that he now found his early dichotomy between the world and the monastery, a dominant theme in all his early works and especially in *The Seven Storey Mountain,* most distasteful. "I was still dealing in a crude theology that I had learned as a novice," he said, "a clean-cut division between the natural and supernatural, God and the world, sacred and secular." In fact, he spent the last years of his life consciously trying to live down his "Seven Storey Mountain" image.[30]

The third period began in May 1949, when he was ordained to the priesthood, and it ended in 1955, when he was made master of the Choir Novices. Soon after his ordination his health gave way for the second time since entering the monastery, and he was unable to write for some eighteen months. He later explained the effect that this illness had upon his writings: "It takes more than good will to write a book. What you write has to come up out of the depths of your being and if, in those depths, the instinct for self-expression has dried up or become paralyzed, there is no way of writing a book. I should say, there is no way of writing a good book. In this state of intellectual siege I might, quite possibly, have written a bad book."[31] But as soon as he had regained his health he began to write again with renewed zeal, and the next few months were a time of immense productivity in which he completed the writing and editing of three major prose works in less than a year: *Bread in the Wilderness, The Ascent to Truth,* and *The Sign of Jonas.* For *The Ascent to Truth* the Catholic

Writers Guild gave him the Golden Book Award for the best spiritual book written by an American writer in 1951.

Then in 1951 Merton was appointed Master of the Scholastics, which made him responsible for the education of young monks studying for ordination, and the books which he wrote between 1951 and 1955 grew out of the classes in theology which he conducted. They were primarily concerned with the spiritual life and methods of contemplation, but throughout they hinted at a new awareness of the world outside the walls, a world perhaps brought back to Merton's attention by the new monks who were still attached to the society which they had so recently departed. Among these books were *The Living Bread, No Man Is an Island, The Silent Life, A Balanced Life of Prayer, The Strange Islands,* and *Thoughts in Solitude.*

The fourth period began in 1955 when he became Master of the Choir Novices and ended in 1965 when he was permitted at last to lay aside his duties after twenty-four years of service and become a hermit. During those eleven years his heavy load of responsibilities did not permit him to write long books, and the ones that he did write were collections of smaller works, written separately but on common themes and finally united under single titles. These books reveal a new Merton, one who was as interested in nuclear war as in solitude, as involved in Oriental mysticism as in Catholic liturgy. Some of these books are *Disputed Questions, Behavior of Titans, New Seeds of Contemplation, Redeeming the Times, Seeds of Destruction, Original Child Bomb, Emblems of a Season of Fury, Gandhi on Non-Violence, The Way of Chuang-tzu, Raids on the Unspeakable, Mystics and Zen Masters,* and *Conjectures of a Guilty Bystander.* Merton felt that the writings in this fourth period were the most significant of his entire career, for they dealt with the problems of contemporary society and therefore symbolized to him a "successful attempt to escape the limitations that I inevitably created for myself with *The Seven Storey Mountain.*" They represented a "refusal to be content with the artificial public image which this autobiography created." These books greatly expanded Merton's audience by permitting him to cross the boundaries of his own church and speak to a larger public.

The fifth period began in 1965 when, after almost a quarter of a century at Gethsemani, he was permitted to retire from his assigned writings, speaking engagements, and teaching duties. He took up residence in a cinderblock cabin deep in the monastery's woods and lived as a hermit for three years until his death in 1968. At noon each day he would walk the half-mile to the abbey, say mass, eat his one community meal of the day, and fill his bucket with cold water for washing and shaving. Otherwise, he spent his time writing what he pleased and praying.[32] He lived a simple life filled with contemplation, liturgical prayer, study, and physical exercise such as chopping wood and taking long walks in the woods and valleys. He lived the contemplative vocation in all its purity and strictness and remained essentially a recluse, yet he continued his dialogue with the world and even expanded his worldly studies to include Asian religions, especially Zen Buddhism.[33] His *Zen and the Birds of Appetite* is an excellent testimony to this increasing fascination with the Orient.

He appeared to have found true happiness in his last three years, as any of his few visitors during those years will attest. His time was mostly his own to invest as he felt God wanted him to, and the dialogues that he established proved to be more satisfying than any he had previously known. He succeeded in throwing off the image of a young man who hated the world while retaining his vocation of silence and solitude. His last books, social commentaries such as *Faith and Violence* and avant-garde poetry about American life and world inhumanity such as *Cables to the Ace* and *The Geography of Lograire,* reveal the heady creativity of those days. He was speaking to the world from which he was separated in body but not in spirit, and that world was listening and responding. He was saying what he had always wanted to say but in a way much freer, more human, more compassionate than before.

His interest in Asian religions and the Catholic witness in Asia continued to grow, and the new openness within the church after Vatican II gave him the opportunity to visit Thailand for ecumenical talks with exiled Tibetan Buddhists as well as Asian Cistercians. He left Gethsemani in September 1968, not knowing that his monastic life was ending. After an eight-day retreat with the Tibetan monks, a series of ecumenical conferences with representatives of several religions, and a long conversation with the Dalai Lama, he wrote back to his American friends: "In my contacts with these new friends, I also feel a consolation in my own faith in Christ and his indwelling presence. I hope and believe he may be present in the hearts of all of us."[34]

Merton made his formal address to the ecumenical conference in Bangkok on the morning of December 10, 1968. The speech, called "Marxist Theory and Monastic Theoria," was a long, rambling expression of his great knowledge of the world and love for its people. After speaking he retired to his room for the afternoon, expecting to return for an evening's conference at which time he would appear on a panel to answer questions. Sometime in the afternoon he accidentally touched an exposed electric wire on a fan and was electrocuted. A cry was heard in the other rooms, but no one came immediately to help. His friends back home would later be amazed when they read the unconsciously prophetic words with which he ended his last speech: "So I will conclude. I believe the plan is to have all the questions for this morning's conference this evening at the panel, so I will disappear."[35] Some would remember that he concluded *The Seven Storey Mountain* with the belief that God had called him to Gethsemani in order that he might become "the brother of God and learn to know the Christ of the burnt men,"[36] and that in *Cables to the Ace* he had written:

> Oh the blue electric palaces of polar night
> Where the radiograms of hymnody
> Get lost in the fan![37]

And so he died, twenty-seven years and half his life since entering Gethsemani Abbey on December 10, 1941. His best books were just being published, and his greatest works would have been written in those next twenty years that should have been but will not be his. But even in death his influence increased. If one of its more articulate delegates is correct, the spirit of openness and concern that Merton demonstrated at the Bangkok conference has and will affect all Roman Catholic work in Asia.[38]

Merton was returned to Gethsemani before Christmas and there received a burial suitable for a man of his public stature who was after all still a simple monk. His funeral, a two-hour ceremony written especially for him and filled with alleluias, was a mass celebrated simultaneously by twenty-eight monks dressed in white robes. Louie, as the monks called him, was buried near the chapel, his grave marked in the traditional way with a simple white cross.

Chapter Two

The World &
Thomas Merton

Because Thomas Merton's fame both inside and outside the church reached its height in 1949 with the success of *The Seven Storey Mountain,* many people still think of him as the brilliant young world traveler and poet who left the world and its problems behind forever when he stole away to the knobs of Kentucky. Indeed, Merton created and perpetuated this image during the late 1940s and early 1950s by constantly repeating his characteristic call for Christians to renounce the world's values, abandon man's society, and choose lives of stern and silent devotion to God either in a monastery or in a job that permitted the maximum freedom from secular demands.

But in the late 1950s a new series of books began to issue from Gethsemani Abbey, books filled with expressions of intelligent concern for the world, books that seemed to understand and sympathize with man's problems, books written to everyone's surprise by the Thomas Merton of "Seven Storey Mountain" fame. By the mid-1960s his attitude toward the world had changed so dramatically that Merton-watchers were speaking of the "early Merton" and the "later Merton" to distinguish between his two careers, the one as a silent mystic who celebrated the virtues of monastic life in glowing prose and poetry, the other as a social commentator of great skill and imagination. While these two periods cannot be delineated as precisely as some observers have thought, Merton's attitude toward the world outside the enclosure walls did change during the 1950s, and his reading audience was significantly affected. Some who would never have been attracted to his teachings in 1949 because of their emphasis upon renouncing the world became his loyal admirers in the 1960s because of his social consciousness and concern, while many of his early devotees rejected the new Merton because the romantic aura of separateness which they had so admired was no longer apparent.

The change was not abrupt, taking almost a decade to complete, but it was real enough and is now obvious to anyone who compares *The Seven Storey Mountain* to one of his later publications such as *Seeds of Destruction* or *Faith and Violence*. While he never abandoned his belief in the absolute necessity of monastic separation for some men and in the advisability of his own seclusion, and while he never really altered his pessimistic analysis of the world's condition, he did arrive at a new understanding of himself and his role in society. He began to listen to the world and then to address himself to its problems, referring to himself as a "guilty bystander" who now wanted to help the world find its way through the dark days of racial strife and international disorder.

By 1960 he was no longer the raptured young monk, newly converted to Catholicism, trying to make all Americans share his new faith and naively prescribing the contemplative life as a panacea for all of man's woes. His emphasis had shifted decidedly from the otherworldly to the this-worldly, and he was no longer counseling Christians to leave the world to its own self-destruction and seek personal happiness in contemplation but was rather encouraging them to work within the world for society's redemption. He had become involved in the activities of the world and had come to feel himself an integral part of it, not an alien trapped in it.

Merton's early attitude toward the world and its problems can perhaps best be seen in *The Seven Storey Mountain,* in which he described his initial experiences with the Trappists. Upon arriving at Gethsemani Abbey for Easter retreat in 1941, Merton felt that he had found a place of true order which contrasted vividly with the disorder of the world outside, and he spoke of the sense of peace which filled his heart when he heard the great gate close behind him, shutting out that world.[1] He was so inspired by the purity of monastic life that at the end of his retreat, when he returned to Louisville, he was depressed by the corruption that he saw in man's society. When he became a novice in December of that year he indicated that he never wanted to see the world again and that he would never again concern himself with problems outside the abbey's walls. By choosing the cloister he in fact rejected an opportunity to be a social worker in Harlem, thereby affirming his belief that contemplation was superior to social involvement and declaring that for him the two vocations were mutually exclusive.

Late in 1947, after the publication of numerous poems in praise of monastic devotion, he published his first official statement on the contemplative life, an article entitled "Active and Contemplative Orders." This article accurately reflects Merton's early attitude toward the world by declaring that the contemplative life was the only real Christian vocation. All men, he said, are called to become one with Christ in the heated furnace of contemplative withdrawal from the world and then to go forth and fan the flame which Christ came to kindle; everyone is called to the summit of perfection, to be a contemplative, and to pass on the fruit of his contemplation to others.[2] He explained that by prayer and meditation he himself had picked some of the fruit of contemplation and that his obligation as a Christian contemplative was to share this spiritual food with the world. He was concerned about the condition of man's society, but he seemed to believe that his own task was to minister to its spiritual, not its social needs.

Merton's early writings all expressed this same basic spiritual approach to social problems, an approach that could be found in the contemporary works of Bishop Fulton Sheen, Norman Vincent Peale, and Billy Graham, the popular religious writers and lecturers of the day. Each of these men, riding the same wave of postwar religious euphoria, had his own personal approach to religion (Merton's was contemplation), but none of them seemed to understand or speak to social issues, all emphasizing the need for and the possibility of a great spiritual revolution that would cure society's sicknesses without mentioning the necessity of a painful social revolution as well.

In 1948 Merton published his history of the Trappist order—a major work entitled *The Waters of Siloe.* The very title of this book discloses his attitude toward monastic and secular life during the late 1940s when he was collecting, organizing, and writing his history, for in his preface he explains that the waters of Siloe, the waters of peace, are the spiritual dividends to be gained from living the contemplative life. He even implies that only the strict world of Trappist silence can give man this peace. At the time that this book was being written the Trappists were in the midst of a period of rapid growth, receiving more volunteers than ever before, and Merton asked his readers: Why are the healthiest, most energetic and optimistic of America's young men shaving their heads, putting on robes, working in the fields of an abbey, praying half the night, and sleeping on straw? His own answer, which emerged as he related the history and described the life of the Trappists, was that these young men were becoming monks, and especially Trappists, because the Trappist life, of all monastic and secular lives, least resembled "the life which men lead in the towns and cities of our world." He said: "They have not come to the monastery to escape from the realities of life but to find these realities; they have felt the terrible insufficiency of life in a civilization that is entirely dedicated to the pursuit of shadows."[3]

Merton theorized that the Trappists had survived and actually increased their number primarily because they were the most authentically monastic of the orders; that is, because they had been able to free themselves more and more from the active missions of teaching and preaching: "The order has recovered its full strength in proportion as it has withdrawn from fields of endeavor into which it never had any business to go. In other words, a contemplative community will prosper to the extent that it is what it is meant to be, and shuts out the world, and withdraws from the commotion and excitement of the active life, and gives itself entirely to penance and prayer."[4] While he also argued that the contemplative cares for his fellowman, he implies in the text that the contemplative really cares only about man's spiritual salvation, not about his earthly condition. Thus in 1948 Merton seemed to feel that his responsibility toward his fellowman was purely spiritual, and his writings at that time contained no analysis of or suggested solutions for the problems of the world. The monk's job, he said, is "to empty himself of all that is selfish and turbulent and make way for the unapprehended Spirit of God." This he believed was his own ministry, in fact his whole life.

In 1949, the year in which *The Seven Storey Mountain* became the number three best seller of the year, Merton also published *Seeds of Contemplation,* a book of beautiful meditations on the contemplative life, which he modestly but incorrectly claimed could have been written by anyone involved in monastic pursuits. The book was almost entirely mystical in composition and outlook, and except for one isolated comment about the bomb and one about Karl Marx it could have been written by a medieval monk.[5] Although Merton was born in the twentieth century and knew a good deal about the twentieth-century world, this book about prayer in the sunny fields of a Trappist abbey contained little more reference to contemporary events than if the author had died in the thirteenth. *The Seven Storey Mountain* itself, although hailed as a great literary creation, was criticized by a number of Catholic leaders and even by some monks for its unnecessarily heavy emphasis upon renunciation to the neglect of social involvement. But *The Seven Storey Mountain* and *Seeds of Contemplation* attracted a large audience of admirers, the largest of his career, and established his popular image as the silent monk who cared little about man's society.

In 1951 there appeared *The Ascent to Truth,* a commentary on the life of Saint John of the Cross, in which Merton sought to formulate a theology of contemplation. While the book did indicate that he was beginning to think more about the contemplative's relationship to the world, it did not approach an adequate description of the social implications of the monastic life. He was still calling for a great spiritual revolution which he felt would save the world from moral collapse, believing that this revolution would come just as soon as Christians rediscovered the traditional practices of contemplation, asceticism, mental prayer, and otherworldliness.[6] Aware of the criticism being leveled against *The Seven Storey Mountain* and *Seeds of Contemplation* for their exclusive otherworldliness, their portrayal of the monk as the most religious of Christians, and their failure to do justice to the Christian command to redeem the times, he added to *The Ascent to Truth* a note to the effect that rejecting the world's standards does not incapacitate a Christian for social action in the world, that contemplation is in fact an essential prerequisite for Christian social service. He still showed no evidence, however, of having devised an adequate social corollary to his theology of contemplation. Much later in his career he would give prayer and social action equal importance in the achievement of perfection, but in *The Ascent to Truth* prayer was still given a vastly superior status.

In spite of the public image being created by these books, however, the journals which Merton kept during the late 1940s and early 1950s and the book of theological meditations *No Man Is an Island* indicate that his opinion concerning the relationship between the monastery and the world was beginning to change. The change was a slow one, involving a long process of rethinking his presuppositions and of learning to express his new way of thinking; not until the late 1950s did he fully assume the role of social commentator, but the process of reevaluation had evidently begun as early as 1950. Although *No Man Is an Island* revealed no real knowledge or understanding of the world outside the abbey, its title and prologue indicate that through his experiences in the monastery Merton had discovered his need for other men and a responsibility to them. Several examples of this change can be found in the journal that he kept between 1946 and 1952, published in 1953 as *The Sign of Jonas.*

In one paragraph, written in 1949 just after his ordination, he stated that the responsibilities of his priesthood had taught him the meaning of self-sacrifice, that when he said mass he belonged to mankind. In a later paragraph, after some months of teaching the young monks as Master of Scholastics, he wrote that he had found his long-desired hermitage by coming to know his students better. When he knew his brothers less intimately, he explained, he let them stand in the way of his solitude; now that he knew them better, he felt with them a common desire for God which made him both responsible for them and free of them.

Also during this period he reread "Journal of My Escape from the Nazis," a manuscript which he had written in the early 1940s and which was published posthumously as the novel *My Argument with the Gestapo.* In 1941 he had expressed the opinion that "the whole world, of which the war is a characteristic expression, is evil" and that it should be ridiculed, spat upon, and finally rejected with a curse, but when he read the manuscript again in 1951 he realized that he felt quite differently about a number of things. He now felt that the only reason for becoming a monk was to find his true place in the world and that if he should withdraw so far into the monastic life that he lost his place in society he would be wasting his time. He went on to rebuke himself for his earlier hatred and rejection of the world and to conclude that it is a grave sin to curse the evil in the world without praising the good that is there also. He even laughed at himself for withdrawing from the world and writing pious books about how different he was. The Thomas

Merton of "Journal of My Escape from the Nazis" was an immobile nonentity, he said, a product of psychological withdrawal, and it was time for a new Thomas Merton to emerge.[7]

This startling change in attitude, just beginning in 1951, eventually made Merton one of the church's most outspoken social critics, and his books and articles in the 1960s revealed a thinker totally immersed in the problems of the world, a monk who was very much a man of the twentieth century. Apparently during the decade following the writing of *The Seven Storey Mountain* his attitude toward his own role in the world underwent a significant shift, and the Merton of the 1960s, while not irreconcilable with the Merton of the 1940s, was a different man. One particular article, written in 1966 and entitled "Is the World a Problem?" illustrates Merton's new attitude and his own awareness of his change. He began by saying that he wanted very much to destroy the stereotype of young Tom Merton, the man who had "spurned New York, spat on Chicago, and tromped on Louisville, heading for the woods with Thoreau in one pocket, John of the Cross in another, and holding the Bible open at the Apocalypse."[8] Denying that he was still the same man who wrote *The Seven Storey Mountain,* he said he wished to be known simply as a self-questioning person:

> I am . . . a man in the modern world. In fact, I *am* the world just as you are! Where am I going to look for the world first of all if not in myself?
> As long as I imagine that the world is something to be "escaped" in a monastery—that wearing a special costume and following a quaint observance takes me "out of this world," I am dedicating my life to an illusion.[9]

And in 1967 he told an interviewer from *Motive* magazine: "I was still dealing in a crude theology that I had learned as a novice: a clean-cut division between the natural and supernatural, God and the world, sacred and secular, with boundary lines that were supposed to be quite evident. Since those days I have acquired a little experience, I think, and have read a few things, tried to help other people with their problems—life is not as simple as it once looked in *The Seven Storey Mountain."*[10]

Thus it is quite clear that Merton's attitude toward the world and his place in it underwent a dramatic change during the 1950s, moving from spiritual isolationism to involvement in the affairs of contemporary man. Although he did not leave the monastery or stop advising Christians to practice silence and contemplation, he did once again turn his eyes upon the world he had left behind and entered into dialogue with its citizens. His pilgrimage is in fact a microcosmic illustration of H. Richard Niebuhr's interpretation of the history of American religious thought. Niebuhr said that while the ideal and goal of American religion has always been the kingdom of God, the definition of "kingdom" has constantly been modified. To the Puritan it would be found by following a sovereign God into the wilderness of New England; to nineteenth-century revivalists it would come by converting men's hearts to the way of Christ; to advocates of the social gospel in recent times it would be realized when the society was reformed and redeemed. Just as American religious history moved from subjection to a sovereign God to spiritual evangelism to active social redemption, so Thomas Merton's life moved from withdrawal into the wilderness at the command of a sovereign God who had given up on the world, to an attempt to save his fellowman's soul through "spiritual" writings, to social criticism aimed at redeeming his fellowman's world.

Perhaps the most important factor in Merton's change was Thomas Merton himself, an honest man who was always responsive to a new idea that might increase his awareness and understanding of life, a man who was therefore willing to change his mind when the evidence indicated that he should. He was always more creative than systematic, more a poet than a theologian, and he always viewed himself and his work as critically as possible, willing to change directions when he saw an error in his thinking, as he did when his monastic studies and teaching and his trips into town gave him the opportunity. He is in fact something of a problem for his more systematically oriented interpreters, for his openness and willingness to change, his ability to see always another side of an issue, his oriental insight into the dual and somewhat ambivalent nature of reality, created a contradictory system of thought. And added to these problems is the fact that Merton seemed to publish his every waking and sleeping thought in one form or another, bringing into the open his every intellectual ambivalence and conceptual metamorphosis. His was no small mind, and it housed no such hobgoblins as the drive for detailed consistency. A meditation, written on New Year's Eve 1950 best illustrates his spirit of self-examination, honesty, and flexibility.

He was sitting on a plank by an old barn in the pasture near the monastery's enclosure wall, examining his conscience, when he spied two hunters and a dog in the orchard beyond the wall. After watching them for some time he came to understand that the hunt was an act, that neither the men nor the dog really wanted to find a rabbit, and that the barking and loud talking, the jumping upon the wall to wait for rabbits to run by, and the aiming of the gun were all part of the act. When the "hunters" became aware of the "monk" watching them, Merton began to ask himself whether he should act out his own part by shaking his fist at them to get off his wall, but he finally decided just to sit still, appearing to have good will toward the world but unwilling to get involved in it, as a good monk. He mused: "So there we stay. He stands on top of the wall 'hunting' and I sit on a board, 'meditating.' I have a book with me. He has a gun. Both are factors in a disguise." The hunters did not know who Merton was, and he did not know who they were, and he wondered whether either of them knew who he himself was. He concluded in his typically honest way: "And that leaves me in the presence of an immense difficulty—the task of asking myself if I am a monk in the same way as he is a hunter, and if so, if this should be a cause for alarm."[11] The ability to question himself, to examine his conscience, as revealed by this simple story, explains how Merton was able to move from one emphasis to another, to remain flexible and creative in his thinking, to change his attitude toward the world and his own place in it.

But Merton's honesty and openness could never have led him to change his attitude so completely had it not been for a liberalization of the Trappist order in general and Gethsemani Abbey in particular in the late 1940s. Had the rules not been changed to permit the monks more freedom, he might never have met the world again and might never have had an opportunity to respond in a creative fashion. Merton once explained to me that for the first few years of his monastic life the rules were so strict that the monks had little time for social issues, spending all their time in worship and in trying to remain healthy. He said that his first abbot, Dom Frederic Dunne, was a very strict and traditional Trappist who believed a monk should not involve himself in worldly activities. Under his rule the monks never went outside the walls and received almost no news from the outside world, learning the details of the atomic attack upon Hiroshima, for example, several months after the event. They prayed in an unheated chapel until the late 1940s in below-freezing weather, sometimes got as little as three hours sleep at night, and received an insufficiently nourishing diet. Merton's own body reacted negatively to those harsh conditions, and he became ill with a respiratory disease that was at first incorrectly diagnosed as tuberculosis. It was only after the reforms, some of which awaited the arrival of Merton's second abbot, Dom James Fox, that Merton discovered that he needed the world and the world needed him. He admitted then that his earlier attitude had been both limited and inadequate, if not downright wrong and even a bit sinful.[12] In *New Seeds of Contemplation,* a complete revision of the original *Seeds of Contemplation,* he admitted that when he wrote the first version he was an isolated monk who had not confronted the needs and problems of other men. As early as 1950 he had written in *No Man Is an Island* that the monk, to be a true saintly servant of God, must see himself as part of man's society, but several years would pass before he could become well enough reacquainted with that society to be its servant.

When the reforms at Gethsemani permitted him to renew his acquaintance with man's society, Merton discovered that he loved that which he once had hated. This emotional revision began in 1948 when he was asked to accompany his French-speaking vicar general, Dom Gabriel Sortais, to Louisville as his translater. He had not been away from the monastery since December 1941, and he wondered how he would react to the world after seven years in the cloister, but soon he realized how radically he had changed. The disgusted young man of twenty-six who had entered the monastery to escape the war-torn world was now a mature monastic brother of thirty-three who, having made peace with himself, could now accept the world as it was. He wrote in his journal: "I wondered how I would react at meeting once again, face to face, the wicked world. I met the world and I found it no longer so wicked after all. Perhaps the things I had resented about the world when I left it were defects of my own that I had projected upon it. Now, on the contrary, I found that everything stirred me with a deep and mute sense of compassion." He admitted that most of the people he saw were the same rough, Midwestern types of individuals that he had been glad to leave behind seven years earlier, but, he added, "I did not stop to observe it [their appearance] because I seemed to have lost an eye for merely external detail and to have discovered, instead, a deep sense of respect and love and pity for the souls that such details never fully reveal. I went through the city, realizing for the first time in my life how good are all the people in the world and how much value they have in the sight of God."[13]

Merton's experience in the monastery was allegorically similar to the experience of the man in Plato's cave who, freed from his chains, rushed out into the sunlight and, though blinded for some time by the brightness, eventually recovered his sight, learned about the real world, and finally returned to the cave to help other men slip out of their chains. Merton rushed out of what to him was the shadowy world of New York City into the monastery, his "real world" of light, was blinded for a time by the new-found reality, and only after a few years of adjustment and maturity turned once again to the task of helping his fellowman. But it is also true that after entering the monastery to free himself of the world's illusions he found that the illusions were just as much in himself and in the monastic life as in man's world, and because of this discovery he turned again to the world in a humble attempt to share the truth with his fellowman. In his monastic experience he had learned that he and his fellowman were one in nature and destiny.

He began to leave the monastery more frequently after 1948, and with each encounter he came to love the people in the world more. He saw their needs, studied their problems, and began to discuss these needs and problems, first in conversations with his visitors and then in his writings. During one trip to the city in 1957 he had what can be described as a mystical experience in his new confrontation with the world. He wrote: "In Louisville, at the corner of Fourth and Walnut, in the center of the shopping district, I was suddenly overwhelmed with the realization that I loved all those people, that they were mine and I theirs, that we could not be alien to one another even though we were total strangers. It was like waking from a dream of separateness, of spurious self-isolation in a special world, the world of renunciation and supposed holiness."

He said that he could see the secret beauty of those people's hearts, the place where sin could not reach, and he felt that he saw them as God sees them. He believed that if all men could see themselves as he saw them that day there would be no more greed, cruelty, or war. He was fully aware of being one of them and was overjoyed at the idea. "This sense of liberation from an illusory difference was such a relief and such a joy to me that I almost laughed out loud. And I suppose my happiness could have taken form in the words: 'Thank God, thank God that I am like other men, that I am only a man among others.' To think that for sixteen or seventeen years I have been taking seriously this pure illusion that is so much of our monastic thinking."[14]

Each time Merton ventured out of his walls of silence his interest in and love for the world, with all its poverty and confusion, increased, and his later social commentaries, *Disputed Questions, Seeds of Destruction, Conjectures of a Guilty Bystander,* and *Faith and Violence,* were the full bloom of a slowly germinating seed which was planted on the road to Louisville in 1948. One of these trips, on June 22, 1951, was particularly significant for his theological and social development. On that day he visited the Federal District Court and became a citizen of the United States, following a ceremony in which he answered questions about his membership in the socialist National Students League, recited the oath of allegiance, and received a flag from a delegation of Daughters of the American Revolution. His first trip to Louisville in 1948 had caused him to love the people of America and to be concerned about them. This trip caused him to love and to be concerned about the nation itself. He wrote in his journal that for the first thirty-six years of his life he had been proud of his freedom from national identity, thinking that by simply throwing away his earthly passport he would become a citizen of heaven, but that now he felt the naturalization board, by making him a citizen of the United States, had helped to make him a citizen of the kingdom of God.

He was soon saying that his nationality had a meaning in the light of eternity. He came to believe that perhaps it was his task to "objectify the truth that America, for all its evil, is innocent and somehow ignorantly holy," and he said that at long last he was willing to accept himself as he was, the monastery as it was, and America as it was, "atomic bomb and all."[15] The many books and articles which Merton wrote after the mid-1950s on such social issues as war, the bomb, racial conflict, and communism may well have had their origin in his oath of allegiance to the United States taken in 1951, for as an American citizen he came to feel more and more responsible for his country's salvation and perfection.

From the time Merton became a citizen of the United States he began to take seriously the task of redeeming American society, particularly trying to protect Americans both from themselves and from those who might exploit them. In his "Letter to an Innocent Bystander" he explained his involvement in social affairs by telling his fellow intellectuals that there are basically three groups in American society: They, the ones who seek to establish power over their fellowmen; the Others, those who are helpless and can easily be controlled by Them; and We, the intellectuals who are in the middle and must protect the Others from Them. We, he explained, must recognize Them and expose Them before They set up their machinery and secret police.[16] He asserted that it was not "honorable to stand by as the helpless witness of a cataclysm, with no other hope than to die innocently and by accident, as a nonparticipant." In fact, he labeled the witness to a crime who simply stands aside, telling himself that he is an innocent bystander, an accomplice to the crime. The intellectual, even if he is a monk, must step out of his lethargic pattern and get involved in all the struggles of the Others, he said, for there is in reality no such thing as an innocent bystander.

He reminded his fellow intellectuals of the story of "The Emperor's New Clothes" in which a tailor told the people that only good men could see the ruler's new clothes and thereby tricked everyone in the kingdom into pretending that they saw the nonexistent clothes. Even the emperor pretended to see the clothes until a child, in innocent honesty, pointed out that there were no clothes, that the ruler was in fact naked. Merton applied this parable to contemporary society and his own place in it: "Have you and I forgotten that our vocation, as innocent bystanders—and the very condition of our terrible innocence—is to do what the child did, and keep on saying the king is naked, at the cost of being condemned criminals? If the child had not been there, they would all have been madmen or criminals. It was the child's cry that saved them."[17] Although he and his fellow monks and fellow intellectuals (not necessarily, but for all practical purposes, mutually exclusive groups) were limited in power, they did possess the clarity of vision and hopefully the honesty and courage to save American and world society.

Merton's sense of responsibility for America coincided with the experience of many other Catholics in the United States during this period. After World War II Catholics, because of their rapid growth in size and influence, ceased to be a minority group, and many who had heretofore thought of themselves as immigrants successfully threw off their "ghetto mentality" to accept the responsibilities of full citizenship. Nothing contributed more to this change in attitude among Catholics, Thomas Merton included, than the election of John F. Kennedy to the presidency of the United States. Kennedy was the first Catholic president, elected just thirty-two years after the defeat of Alfred E. Smith, the first Catholic nominee for president, in a campaign tainted with religious bigotry. Many Catholics who had not participated fully in the American national movement, Merton among them, now began to take full cognizance of their responsibilities toward serving the nation and its citizens.

There are indications that Merton's admiration for Kennedy had a profound effect upon his attitude toward American society. In one journal entry he said that he had just read Kennedy's inaugural address and believed the nation had a good, well-intentioned president, a president whom he could advise his friends to respect and follow.[18] He often commented on Kennedy's social reforms and his handling of foreign affairs, especially the Cuban Missile Crisis in 1962, and appeared to be well read on Kennedy's activities. He had more sympathy with Kennedy's handling of domestic and international affairs, particularly the war in Viet Nam, than with Lyndon Johnson's handling of them.[19]

Merton's sense of social responsibility is illustrated also by a manuscript introducing his translation of several essays written by Fenelon, tutor to the Duke of Burgundy, heir of Louis XIV of France. Although Merton did not specifically say so, he seems to have considered himself and other intellectuals and monks to be modern-day Fenelons. He introduced his translation by explaining that the author had lived at Versailles and had observed firsthand the autocratic policies of the power-hungry Louis; he had realized that power politics such as those he saw could lead to the ruin of France and of all Europe, and he had consciously tried to lead his young charge in another direction.[20] Hoping to make of the young duke a truly Christian king, he had composed a number of treatises to aid in formulating his political conscience, always interpreting history and political theory in terms of Christian ethics and according to the standards of Christian morality.

Merton's intense interest in the life and work of Fenelon was doubtless due in part to his feeling of kinship with this moralist who advised political leaders. Like Fenelon, Merton saw himself as something of a spiritual adviser to the leaders of a nation in trouble, to leaders who did not necessarily welcome his counsel. Fenelon, by addressing himself to the social problems of his day in his role as a priest, justified Merton's own assumption of the role of social prophet. Even the titles of Fenelon's essays which Merton translated agree in sentiment with the topics that he himself discussed during the last ten years of his own life: "Even Just Wars Are Evil," "War Is Armed Robbery," "The Tyrant Destroys His Own Power," and "The Sickness of Affluence."

Important also for Merton's change in attitude was the change in the Roman Catholic Church during the pontificate of John XXIII. In the brief five years of his reign Pope John radically altered the course of church history, converting the attitude of the church from one of smug self-assurance in the face of world conditions that might have destroyed it and mankind to one of openness and concern about the needs of modern man, an attitude clearly mirrored in the writings of the best-known Trappist. Acting in accord with a small but prophetic minority of churchmen, Pope John's ecumenical council attacked the major problems of modern society in such a dynamic way that the image of the church and the attitudes of its members were decisively and permanently altered; many who had thought of the church as the arbiter of absolute theological truth came to think of it rather as God's servant in the world and as God's instrument of redemption for man's social and spiritual life. Merton, a thoughtful and sensitive Catholic, was deeply affected by the church's new statement of faith and set out to fulfill its demands.

He was in fact so impressed by Pope John's encyclical letter *Pacem in Terris* that he wrote an official interpretation and response called "The Challenge of Responsibility." He particularly approved of the pope's request that Catholics move out of their spiritual ghetto and establish meaningful dialogue with non-Catholics. He said that the real question facing the "dwindling and confused Christian minority in the West" was not whether they *could* do anything to improve world conditions, as Pope John commanded, but what they actually intended to do. He believed that Christians could have great influence if they only tried to exercise the powers which they already possessed, for there were many Christians and humanists in places of high importance who would listen if Christians would speak out. Here and elsewhere Merton

echoed the spirit of Pope John when he reminded Christians that
the doctrine of the Incarnation, which teaches that God loved the
world so much that in order to save it he became a man, demands
that the followers of the Incarnate Word also love and help to save
the world.[21] He said, for example, that since Pope John's encyclical
taught Catholics to have an open attitude toward all people and
thereby to avoid narrow nationalism, Catholics should dissent from
the collective opinion of any country which follows policies contradictory to the good of all people in the world. Merton's own
writings and activities seemed at times decidedly anti-American, as
when in 1968 he became spiritual counselor to a young man who
wished to avoid the draft, but his criticism of American actions was
almost always criticism of narrow nationalistic policies, not of
honest attempts to find peace and advance progress.

Pope John's pontificate, which began in 1958 when Merton was
in the process of reevaluating his own responsibility to the world,
inspired him to adopt and develop a new social theology. Because
the pope commanded Catholics to address themselves to political
and social issues, Merton began to discuss current American and
world affairs, at times applauding and at times opposing his own
country's policies but always speaking up for what he thought was
right.

But Merton's change in attitude also had to do with his great
desire to emulate the saints and to become one himself. His several
books on such saints as John of the Cross and on such potential
saints as Mother Berchmans gave him great insight into the charac-
ters of those who reach sainthood, and after his rather lengthy research he began to see that the one characteristic common to all
declared saints, and thus of all saints, is their compassion for mankind. Merton concluded that before a man could become a saint he
must first of all become a man, "in all the humanity and fragility
of man's actual condition."[22] Thus he reasoned: "sanctity is not a
matter of being less human, but more human than other men. This
implies a greater capacity for concern, for suffering, for understanding, for sympathy, and also for humor, for joy, for appreciation of the good and beautiful things of life."[23]

His research into the lives of the saints and the saintly convinced
him that Christian holiness is not a private affair achieved by a
monk who isolates himself from others but rather an integral part
of a larger effort to renew society; the man who wants to be a

saint, he said, must work "to produce conditions in which all men can work and enjoy the just fruits of their labor in peace."[24] He began to read about, correspond with, and pray for the world and its people, and he soon discovered that loving the world was not just a task for the man who wanted to be a saint but the natural and most healthy center of human life and activity.

And Merton's movement from renunciation to involvement in world affairs was also affected by the sharp decline in monastic volunteers in the late 1950s. One of his strongest and most frequent arguments for the validity of the monastic vocation and Christian contemplation in the early days had been the tremendous increase in the number and sizes of monasteries in the United States. Between 1944 and 1957 the Trappists alone built nine new monasteries, and by 1955 they could count one thousand full-time members in the United States. By 1968, however, their membership was down to five hundred with no end to the decline in sight.[25] This decline, quite natural after the postwar disillusionment that led so many sensitive men to become monks began to wane, may well have made Merton realize that he must speak to the world where it was rather than simply call it to himself. Some critics of monastic reform have said that the liberalization of Trappist abbeys, their new openness to the world, caused their decline, but the decline itself demonstrated to Merton the need for liberalization.

One of Merton's statements from *The Sign of Jonas* seems to sum up his experiences in the monastic life: "Coming to the monastery has been for me exactly the right kind of withdrawal. It has given me perspective. It has taught me how to live. And now I owe everyone else in the world a share in that life. My first duty is to start, for the first time, to live as a member of a human race which is no more (and no less) ridiculous than I am myself. And my first human act is the recognition of how much I owe everybody else."[26]

While Merton never doubted that his decision to become a monk was right for him and always retained his separation and silence, he gradually came to realize that only by loving and helping to save his fellowman in the world could he be a true monk. His ability to redefine his own role in society, the opportunity for this redefinition, and the ultimate success of his attempt to find a more perfect way of serving God and his fellowman are tributes to Merton, his church, his order, and the contemplative life.

Chapter Three

The Social Ethics
of Contemplation

Being a fallible man, Thomas Merton made many errors in judgment during his years as a spokesman for the contemplative life, and although he corrected most of them as his thought matured, they helped create a false image of his personality and attitude. In his early writings, for example, he unconsciously gave the impression that contemplation in the monastic sense was for everyone and that the monastic life was superior to life in the world. One might catch strong hints of this attitude in *The Seven Storey Mountain* and *Seeds of Contemplation*. He seemed to be tempting the average Christian away from his proper business, which is redeeming the times through living in the world, by calling him to renounce the world and be a contemplative. He gave the reader who shared his own indignation at the world's evils, but who had to live in society, a pleasing sense of being on God's side, and in his condemnation of the unregenerate "they" he came close to assuming a holier-than-thou pose.[1]

But maturity and experience corrected his unexamined attitude. He continued to point out the failures and perversions of the world, but he stopped asking its citizens to become monks, admitting that the contemplative life could be lived in the world by men and women who help to cure the diseases of modern life best by living in society among other men. He came to understand that all men are not equal in their need for, or in their ability to achieve, the deeper levels of the contemplative life, and he began to emphasize the need for contemplative laymen to participate in social action. He rejected the idea that there is one level of holiness for professional contemplatives and another for laymen, warning those who think they have only to remain in a state of grace and be pulled into heaven on the robes of religious specialists that they were in danger of missing the central meaning of the Christian faith.[2] He still called for contemplation, indeed this remained his dominant theme, but he always explained that different people in different situations need different amounts and kinds of contemplation and that one method, especially the monastic one, should not be made standard for all men. By emphasizing previously neglected areas of his thought he was able to clarify and systematize his earlier, somewhat confusing theology of contemplation.

He also tended in the early days of his contemplative life to exaggerate the difference between life in the cloister and life in the world. He saw the world as a distorted parody of God's original creation and the monastery as the most nearly perfect example of true godly society. Such books as *The Strange Islands* gave this impression.[3] But his later definition of true community, while it still pointed out the glaring faults in the world and called upon men both inside and outside the monastery to practice contemplation, did not demand that all good men become monks or even farmers. He came to understand that all men, whatever their jobs or locations, could and must share in the contemplative life if true community were to be achieved and if the world were to be saved. He came to see that there was good in the world as well as in the monastery and that there was much of the world's evil in the church and even in the monastery. He abandoned his superficial Augustinianism, which saw the City of God and the City of Man as distinct and hostile camps, for a deeper, more subtle, and more accurate Augustinianism, which saw the two cities intertwined.

It was only in the latter part of his career that Merton finally achieved what he had worked for all his life: a consistent and reasonable theology of contemplation. He retained the positive elements of the earlier, simpler days and added a great deal of new thought, correcting and tempering the early theology and making it more relevant and helpful for all men, both inside and outside the monastery. Merton's theology of contemplation is important to the layman because on one level he too must be a contemplative; it is important to the professional contemplative because it is his whole life; and it is important to the serious student of Thomas Merton's social theology because it explains why he thought and acted as he did.

Because Merton believed contemplation to be an integral part of the life of anyone, monk, priest, or layman, who wants to carry God's message of spiritual and social redemption to modern man, much of what he said about contemplation applies to anyone who desires to know God and understand God's will better. He encouraged the average man who lives in a city, works among machines, rides the subway, and eats in a cafe where the radio makes him deaf with spurious news to be grateful for his trials; he pointed out that one's very distaste for these trials is a gift from God, a seed of solitude planted in his soul. He suggested that every man, whether in society or in the monastery, set aside a place where no one will disturb him and at a regular time go there for contemplation so that when he returns he can love the world more.[4]

By leading one to God, the Author of man's existence, Merton said, contemplation would give to the monk or the layman, each in his own way and to his own degree, the good life; by helping him discover the basic order of existence through knowledge of God, it would show him the real meaning of his life and thus make life worth living. It would give an order, coherence, and direction to life by leading him into "existential communion with Him Who Is."[5]

It would also help him to find himself. Merton said that every man is imprisoned by a false self almost from the moment of birth and that as he grows older this false self increases in strength and tenacity, overshadowing the true self. Since only God possesses the secret of each person's true identity, one's whole life depends upon meeting in contemplation the God who can remove the false mask and reveal who one really is. Only then does man find true happiness and peace. He explained: "The one true joy on earth is to escape from the prison of our own self-hood (I do not say the body, because the body is God's temple and therefore it is holy), and enter by love into union with the life who dwells and sings within the essence of every creature and in the care of our own souls."[6] He described the release from a false self as a spiritual birth that frees one from the womb of society. While there is a legitimate time for each person to be cozy and warm in the social womb, or the collective myth of man's society, there is also a time to be born, and "he who is spiritually 'born' as a mature identity is liberated from the enclosing womb of myth and prejudice."[7]

Merton discovered from his own contemplative experience that the man who withdraws from society into contemplation, whether it be for a short time or for a lifetime, learns to communicate with his fellowman more effectively than ever before. By learning to communicate with God and with one's own inner being, the true self, one inevitably learns to communicate with other men. Merton's own contemplation prepared him for ecumenical dialogue with Buddhists, Jews, Protestants, and even atheists. He believed that the most fruitful dialogue possible between Christians and Buddhists lay in the area of contemplation. Preparing for his ill-fated trip to the Orient, he said: "While on the level of philosophical and doctrinal formulations, there may be tremendous obstacles to meet, it is often possible to come to a very frank, simple and totally satisfying understanding in comparing notes on the contemplative life, its disciplines, its vagaries, and its rewards."[8] The response to Merton's writings on contemplative prayer bore out the truth of his theory, for they were read and appreciated by men of prayer and meditation in all religions, in spite of differences of theology. Jews who could not accept Merton's Christ and Protestants who could not accept his infallible church were inspired by his spiritual writings.

Merton's contemplation, by helping one communicate with his fellowman, would also help him develop a strong love for him. He believed that when one has entered into solitude, met God, found his own true personality, and learned to live with himself, he knows better how to live with his fellowman and seeks to minister to his needs. Contemplation, Merton believed, is the beginning of true humanism.[9]

Merton came to believe also that true contemplation leads inevitably to social concern and action. When a man is born into the new life of true self-knowledge through contemplation, he said, he may fulfill the obligations of his liberty in one of two ways: by an active life of service to his fellowman with no thought of reward or by a life in the cloister in which, far from being separated from his fellowman in spirit, he becomes every man, suffering all his pain and knowing all his sorrow but also experiencing all his love and joy. Both secular and monastic contemplatives must devote themselves to the world as well as to God, and neither the monastic nor the secular contemplative life is an escape from time, matter, or social responsibility; they are rather "an escape into solitude and the desert, a confrontation with poverty and the void, a renunciation of the empirical self, in the presence of death, and nothingness, in order to overcome the ignorance and error that spring from the fear of 'being nothing.' "[10]

To Merton's way of thinking contemplation not only helps prepare one for social action but actually gives birth to social action by teaching the contemplative that he and his fellowman are one. The discovery of this contemplative ethic during the course of his monastic career led Merton to get involved in world affairs as a social commentator. He believed that the contemplative life cannot be a withdrawal, a negation of the world. Since Christianity is founded upon the historical event of God becoming man in Jesus Christ, the contemplative, whose meditation dwells upon this incarnation, soon finds that he must also become a man and deal with the needs of his fellowman. He is free within time but not free from it. Far from using contemplation as an excuse for rejecting the world, the later Merton found in it a social ethic that demanded the contemplative understand and redeem the world.[11]

But just as the contemplative cannot avoid helping his fellowman, true acts of charity must grow out of contemplation; contemplation leads inevitably to social action, and the most effective social action is born of contemplative prayer. Although Merton believed in "natural" contemplation, the contemplation of the artist who may not even be a Christian, he said that true acts of charity must be fashioned in the light of Christ; otherwise, they represent the deeds of a do-gooder, whom Merton condemned in the spirit of Dante. Because one cannot bring hope and redemption to others unless he possesses hope and redemption himself, Merton reasoned, one must first gain strength and wisdom through contemplation of God before he can share them with others.[12] He explained: "He who attempts to act and do things for others or for the world without deepening his own self-understanding, freedom, integrity and capacity to love, will not have anything to give others."[13]

Merton's contemplative would doubtless see the church in a different light from that of even the noncontemplative Christian. Merton defined Christianity not as a "complex set of ritual observances and ascetic practices," but as above all an "ethic of spontaneous charity" directed to all men as brothers. He thought of all men as his brothers, for they were either members of the Body of Christ or potential members, and he taught that the first rule of the church is to recognize one's need for everyone else and one's obligation to serve everyone else. He wrote:

> Christian charity is meaningless without concrete and exterior acts of love. The Christian is not worthy of his name unless he gives from his possessions, his time, or at least his concern in order to help those less fortunate than himself.
> The sharing of material goods must also be a sharing of the heart, a recognition of common misery and poverty and of brotherhood in Christ. Such charity is impossible without an interior poverty of spirit which identifies us with the unfortunate, the underprivileged, the dispossessed. In some cases this can and should go to the extent of leaving all that we have in order to share the lot of the unfortunate.[14]

By far the most important characteristic of Merton's socially oriented contemplation is that its origin lies in the depths of solitude and silence, in one's psychological desert. Whether the contemplative lives in the city or in the desert, he believed, he invariably lives in solitude, and to some degree he finds himself an isolated conscience opposing the injustice of man's world. He becomes the peculiar person who defends the universal conscience against the mass mind of his society. He is different from his fellowman and thereby reminds him of his true capacity for maturity, liberty, and goodness.[15]

In the early 1940s Merton believed that the contemplative life precluded social concern, but as he matured in thought and experience he became most critical of his early attitude. He came to believe that the monk's traditional contempt for the world and his equally famous rejection of the world were born of a crude, automatic polarity in which everything outside the cloister is regarded as "hateful, ridiculous, erroneous, ungodly, or at least trifling," while everything inside, run according to sacrosanct rules, is "wise, pleasing to God, full of redemptive power, and supremely significant." Monastic contemplatives, he concluded, too often feel that while God is "nauseated by the actions of worldlings outside the cloister," he is consoled by and delighted with "the actions of observant religious within the cloister." Realizing that this distortion of the gospel's command to renounce the world had led him to a kind of pharisaical complacency, Merton sought through his later writings to uproot the common monastic assumption that the world is always bad while the cloister is always good.

He believed that the monk should not even think of the contemplative life as separate from life in the world. The monk should retain his solitude, for it makes him see reality with a clarity that is impossible when completely immersed in the usual cares of life, but he must never forget that he is part of the human race. He should feel that "it is a glorious destiny to be a member of the human race, though it is a race dedicated to many absurdities and one which makes many terrible mistakes: yet with all that, God Himself gloried in becoming a member of the human race."[16]

Merton defended his own attempt to comment on social issues by denying the notion that a monk is a holy, separated individual. While he never questioned the validity of his own vocation or of the monastic life in general, he did reject the theory that a man becomes a different species of being, a pseudo-angel, or even a "spiritual" man by becoming a monk. He believed and taught that the monk, although excluded from the day-to-day activities of the world, is actually in the same world as everyone else. While the monk belongs to God and therefore must take a somewhat different attitude toward all these problems than perhaps the non-Christian or even the Christian might ordinarily be expected to take, he must remember that in the final analysis everyone else belongs to God too. Just because the monk is more conscious of belonging to God and makes a profession of this consciousness, he is not thereby entitled to consider himself different or better than others.[17]

Merton warned that the monk who separates himself completely from his fellowman denies himself the opportunity to achieve the primary aim of the contemplative life, the discovery of his true self, for it is only in communication with both God and other men that this discovery is made. One can never know himself alone. Merton taught that the only genuine justification for entering the monastery is the conviction that his action will help one to love God and his fellowman more, and he urged monastic volunteers to "go into the desert not to escape other men but in order to find them in God."[18] He said: "The ultimate perfection of the contemplative life is not a heaven of separate individuals, each one viewing his own private vision of God: it is a sea of Love which flows through the One Body and Soul of all the elect. . . . the silence of contemplation is deep and rich and endless society, not only with God but with men."[19]

Far from being opposed to each other, he said, internal contemplation and external activity are simply two sides of the same expression of love for God. Even if the monk did not find his own identity in others, even if being near others were of no personal benefit to him, he would still be drawn toward other people by the very nature of the effects of contemplation. He explained: "The more we are alone the more we are together; and the more we are in society, the true society of charity, not of cities and physical mobs, the more we are alone with Him."[20]

True solitude, Merton said, is not the absence of other people but is an abyss in one's own soul from which godly activity comes. The monk is thus not the only contemplative, and the monk who does not find a love for his fellowman in his meditations is not a true contemplative. Perhaps the most explicit and beautiful statement of Merton's definition of the monk's social role is as follows: "We do not go into the desert to escape people but to learn how to find them; we do not leave them in order to have nothing more to do with them, but to find out the way to do them the most good."[21] The true contemplative leaves the world in order to escape self-concern, but rather than escaping his fellowman his newly won freedom helps him to find his fellowman in God. The contemplative's flight from the world is not an escape from conflict, anguish, and suffering; it is rather a "flight from disunity and separation to unity and peace in the love of other men." Therefore, one should become a monk only when he is convinced that such a move will help him to love both God and his fellowman more.[22] As Merton said in "Notes on the Future of Monasticism," monks are "people who have consciously and deliberately adopted a mode of life which is marginal with respect to the rest of society, implicitly critical of that society, seeking a certain distance from the society and a freedom from its domination and its imperatives, but nevertheless open to its needs and in dialogue with it."[23]

Merton believed that a monk serves mankind by being an example, by standing above the false dichotomies of man's secular society and reminding men of the unity that can and will exist for each man in God. The monk, he said, teaches what is real and what is not real, what is true and what is false, for through contemplation of God one discovers reality and truth. Merton felt he had to share his new life with other men through his writings, for he believed that leaving the world to become a monk was actually leaving the false self of pride and selfishness to begin living for others.[24] While as a monk he could not join in the battles that were raging in man's society, he could stand above those battles and divisions and call men back to basic values.[25] There was no foolish pride in Merton's assumption of the role of prophet; he realized that God had called him to the monastery and had given him the aesthetic and intellectual powers to be both a contemplative and a writer, and he was simply fulfilling the obligations of his vocation.

Merton constantly warned those considering monastic careers against trying to escape the world, for one always takes the world along with him. The man who enters the monastic solitude just to be alone simply locks himself up in a private world with his own selfishness and may well lose both his sanity and his soul.[26] He explained that the true contemplative, whose most visible characteristic is his solitude and prayer, must be a participant in the affairs of the world. The two areas of the contemplative's life, the mystical and the social, are so intertwined that he cannot fulfill one without fulfilling the other; the monk must be a man of God and a man of the world.

Merton's most precise statement on the relationship between contemplation and social involvement, a statement which helped to explain his own change in attitude toward the world, was his response to Pope John's encyclical letter *Mater et Magistra*. The Christian, Merton wrote, cannot separate his faith from his works, his life of contemplation from his life in the world. His life with Christ will inevitably affect and in turn be affected by his attitude toward such social problems as the struggle between East and West, race relations, the emergence of new nations, and nuclear war.[27] Genuine holiness is dependent upon a genuine human and social concern, he said, and Christian humanism is not limited to a few esthetes and social reformers; it is "a necessity in the life of every Christian." The concern of the contemplative must go even deeper than the desire for political order and social justice; it must work for the fulfillment of all fundamental human needs: reason, beauty, friendship, affection, protection, order, justice, creative work, food, and rest. In other words, the task of the contemplative Christian is to help provide the basic human values without which grace has no meaning in man's life. The contemplative must protect his fellowman's human dignity from the encroachments of secular society; he must defend man against an ideology in which money and power are considered more important than man himself.[28]

Merton's own attitude toward the world was paradoxical in that the more he learned to love man's society and the more effectively he addressed himself to its problems, the more he felt the need to withdraw from it. He came to believe that in order to serve the world he should separate himself from it, and he felt that to some extent this was true for all Christians. While his concern for the world and his social awareness gave the impression that he was becoming more and more like a Franciscan or Dominican, the more socially oriented orders, his personal life of deeper withdrawal indicated that he was growing more Cistercian, a traditional Trappist.

Perhaps this paradox can be partially explained by saying that Merton believed man's society to be divided into two worlds, not a monastic and a secular division as he had once thought, but the world that destroys man's powers of contemplation and reduces him to a thing and the world of men so victimized.[29] He consistently taught that the contemplative must reject the first and love the second. He described the world which must be rejected by the contemplative, whether in a monastery or in man's society, as "the unquiet city of those who live for themselves and are therefore divided against one another in a struggle that cannot end, for it will go on eternally in hell. It is the city of those who are fighting for possession of limited things and for the monopoly of goods and pleasures that cannot be shared by all."[30] He believed that the contemplative should refuse to take part in this world's activities and delusions, for it is "the image of a society that is happy because it drinks Coca-Cola or Seagrams or both and is protected by the bomb. The society that is imaged in the mass media and in advertising, in the movies, in T.V., in best sellers, in current fads, in all the pompous and trifling masks with which it hides callousness, sensuality, hypocrisy, cruelty, and fear."[31]

While he must reject that world, the "world of mass man," the world in which Merton himself had developed and been imprisoned by a false self-image, he must accept and love the other world, the world of imprisoned men created in the image of God. "Where 'the world' means in fact 'military power,' 'wealth,' 'greed,' then the Christian remains against it. When the world means those who are concretely victims of these demonic abstractions (and even the rich and mighty are their victims too) then the Christian must be for it and in it and with it."[32] Merton taught that the contemplative would indeed learn through his contemplation to love the world of oppressed man, for he would come to see that Christ, the world, his brother, and himself are one. Merton's own later openness toward the world was actually a rewakening to his fellowman, whose problems he sought to understand and solve. He believed that his compassion for man grew in part from his contemplation. Contemplation is the key to Merton's social theory.

From his rich poetic imagination Merton chose two metaphors which served to explain his view of man's world; one symbolized the society with contemplation and one the society without contemplation. The society with contemplation and the acts of social concern which naturally result from it he called the Community. The society without contemplation, the society of men who care neither for God nor their fellowman but only for themselves, he called the City.

The City in Merton's thought was the social order established by men without the aid and counsel of God, and he identified it with several symbolic names from the Bible, church history, and his own experiences, calling it variously Babylon, the Tower of Babel, and his old hometown New York City. The City, he said, leaves its inhabitants with a sense of placelessness and exile, for it is a "ceaseless motion of hot traffic, tired and angry people in a complex swirl of frustration." He continued: "One must move through noise, stink and general anger, through blocks of general dilapidation, in order to get somewhere where anger and bewilderment are concentrated in a neon-lit, air-conditioned enclave, glittering with 'products,' humming with piped-in music and reeking of the sterile and sweet smell of the technologically functioning world."[33]

Merton called man's City a technologically sophisticated monstrosity which shoulders out all God's gifts to man, especially the gift of nature. In an essay entitled "Rain and the Rhinoceros" he contrasted man's attitude toward God's gift of rain in the city and in the country. Whereas rain is a natural festival for the hermit in the woods, it is an annoyance to the urbanite who is caught between buildings, and even though it washes his streets and makes them glisten, he despises the rain because of its inconvenience. The City causes him to reject one of God's loveliest gifts.

Merton dismissed the City as a mere fabrication, a world of buildings in which no natural object can grow freely. If a tree is permitted to grow in the City by a mistake in the architect's blueprints, it is taught to grow with chemicals and given a precise reason for being there. A sign is placed upon it to tell curious observers that it is there for public health, beauty, perspective, peace, or prosperity, or that it was planted by the mayor's daughter. Merton, following the theology of Saint Augustine, believed that the City, its private tree, its buildings, and even its mayor's daughter, are all illusions.

The City dweller loses not only his sense of God's gifts in nature but also his own sense of being a part of God's world. Merton said that the City always bothered his own sleep, depriving him of the natural gift of God which permits a man at peace to float away into the womb of the earth. It was only in his own self-imposed wilderness exile that he had learned to sleep, and he described this sleep: "I close my eyes and instantly sink into the whole rainy world of which I am a part, and the world goes on with me in it, for I am not alien to it. I am alien to the noises of cities, of people, to the greed of machinery that does not sleep, the hum of power that eats up the night."[34]

Merton's most critical indictment of the City was that it confuses man about who he is, opposing the effect of contemplation which reveals man's true identity. The City's society always mistakes the outer shell of the person for the real person, and he is taught to believe that this "personality," which is no more real than the artificial buildings, is really his true self. Because he has been taught that the City can fulfill all his needs, he abandons his natural tendency to rebel against this falsification and permits himself to be molded in this false image so that he can draw upon the collective powers of his society. He conforms to the image which the City gives him to the extent that he even lets it tell him how to dress, what to do for fun, and how to spend his life. He actually comes to believe that this shell is his true identity, that the mask is his own face, and protects this shell with even more fabrications, sometimes losing his own integrity in the process. He will stack fabrication upon fabrication and will become not just a false self but indeed a perversion of man in the image of God.[35] In a late poem Merton portrayed this pathetic creature:

> Whenever he goes to the phone
> To call joy
> He gets the wrong number
> "Man is the saddest animal
> He begins in zoology
> And gets lost
> In his own bad news."[36]

Merton approved of the secular-city movement in contemporary Protestant theology, for he felt that it was a belated but genuine attempt to "transfer Christian insight from the realm of traditional objective theology" to modern man's existential situation. But he rejected what he believed to be the popular interpretation of the movement, a hymn of praise to "American affluence, which is in fact rooted in the enormous military-industrial complex and therefore in the Vietnam war." He believed that the church must reject the City's morality while trying to help it find its way, and he felt that the secular-city theology was in danger of "ending in conformism, acquiescence, and passive approval of the American managerial society, affluent economy and war-making power politics."[37]

Merton in fact even blamed the City for war, which he believed was man's greatest sin and his most dangerous menace. In a somewhat idealized and perhaps totally unverifiable portrayal, he described the primitive, wandering stone-age man as a hunter and farmer who spent all his time with his small family looking for food. Only later, when men began to build cities, did war come to Merton's earth. He believed that "the city is the place where the mythology of power and war develop, the center from which the magic of power reaches out to destroy the enemy and to perpetuate one's own life and riches—interminably if only it were possible."[38]

Among Merton's more striking condemnations of the City is his famous poem "In the Ruins of New York." Here he describes the site of America's greatest city, symbolic of man's City at any time or place, after it has been destroyed by some unspecified force.

> Oh, how quiet it is after the black night
> When flames out of the clouds burned down your cariated teeth,
> And when those lightenings,
> Lancing the black boils of Harlem and the Bronx,

Spilled the remaining prisoners,
(The tens and twenties of the living)
Into the trees of Jersey,
To the green farms, to find their liberty.

Will there be some farmer, think you,
Clearing a place in the woods,
Planting an acre of bannering corn
On the heights above Harlem forest?
Will hunters come explore
The virgin glades of Broadway for the lynx and deer?
Or will some hermit, hiding in the birches, build himself a cell
With the stones of the city hall,
When all the caved-in subways turn to streams
And creeks of fish,
Flowing in sun and silence to the reedy Battery?[39]

But perhaps Merton's most stinging criticism of the City and his most enduring tribute to the Community may be found in his dramatic poem entitled "The Tower of Babel, A Morality." A traditional morality play based upon the destruction of a city, it begins with Merton's instruction to the reader to recite three selections: Genesis 11:1–9 (the story of the tower of Babel which is abandoned when God confuses the tongues); Saint Augustine's *City of God* 14:28 (a comparison of the city of God and the city of man and the difference of their loves); and Revelation 18:21, 23–24 (the announcement of Babylon's fall).

The play's action begins with a group of men busy at the task of building a city tower which they know will fall. Raphael, one of the angelic observers, interprets their plight: "Their hearts seek disaster as a relief from the tedium of an unsatisfactory existence. Ruin will at least divide them from one another. They will be able to scatter, to run away, to put barricades against one another. Since they cannot stand the pretense of unity, they must seek the open avowal of their enmity."[40] The tower and city fall, and the builders are in a state of despair until the Prophet reminds them of the real City which will grow up on the ruins of man's illusory city.

Do not think the destroyed city is entirely evil. As a symbol is destroyed to give place to reality, so the shadow of Babylon will be destroyed to give place to the light which it might have contained. Men will indeed be of one tongue, and they will indeed build a city that will reach from earth to heaven. This new city will not be a tower of sin, but the City of God. Not the wisdom of men shall build this city, nor their machines, nor their power. But the great city shall be built without hands, without labor, without money and without plans.[41]

The Prophet goes on to describe this City of God, which will be the church or, as Merton pictures it in other writings, the Community of contemplation: "It will be a perfect city, built on eternal foundations, and it shall stand forever, because it is built by the thought and the silence and the wisdom and the power of God. But you, my brothers, and I are stones in the wall of this city. Let us run to find our places. Though we may run in the dark, our destiny is full of glory."[42]

As if to illustrate the Prophet's words, the character Thomas points to a distant city built by a clear lake, and the men see the city reflected perfectly in the water. Thomas says: "Look, there are two villages. One, on the shore, is the real village. The other, upside down in the water, is the image of the first. The houses of the real village are solid, the houses in the water are destroyed by the movements in the water, but recreate their image in the stillness that follows."[43] And Raphael the wise explains this phenomenon:

> So it is with our world. The city of men, on earth, is the inverted reflection of another city. What is eternal and unchanging stands reflected in the restless waters of time, and many of the events of our history are simply movements in the water that destroy the temporal shadow of eternity. We who are obsessed with movement, measure the importance of events by their power to unsettle our world. We look for meaning only in the cataclysms which obscure the image of reality. But all the things pass away, and the picture of the real city returns, although there may be no one left to recognize it, or to understand.[44]

Thus Merton used the symbol of the City in much the same way Saint Augustine used the symbol of the city of man; it is the society of men without Christ, who is found in contemplation, and it will inevitably fall. In contrast to the city of man is the city of God, the Community, which will arise from the ashes of man's fallen City when men learn that reality and truth can be found only in contemplation of God.

Merton believed of course that the Community is best exemplified in the monastery, for there all the residents are contemplatives, each retaining his unique human qualities while relating to each other in brotherly love. He pointed to Mount Athos, a peninsula in northern Greece which is an autonomous political unit occupied by monks, as the best example of true political Community. Mount Athos, where the businesses and the government are run by contemplatives who live in the several monasteries, was for Merton the perfect society: a true Community of men whose social affairs are determined and strengthened by contemplation.[45] He also pointed to the Indian cult center Mounte Alban, which he called the first and best city in America, as an example of the beauty and peace possible in a society built around prayer and worship. While only a small number of priests and scholars lived in this pre-Columbian community, large numbers of people from the surrounding area came to help build and perfect the city. Merton saw the monastery as an example of Community life which should be open to all men who wanted to come for retreat and then return to the City to remake it along the lines suggested by the Community.

But the mere fact that men live close together, either in cities or in monasteries, Merton said, is no guarantee that they truly communicate or that they have formed a Community. Although men who live huddled together without true communication appear to share their lives, their so-called communication is really only a common immersion in general meaninglessness. Just as living alone does not necessarily isolate a man, so living together does not necessarily bring men into community. Common life, Merton said, can make a man more or less a person, depending upon whether it is a life of true community, a life lived for others, or simply life in a crowd. He explained: "To live in communion, in genuine dialogue with others, is absolutely necessary if man is to remain human. But to live in the midst of others, sharing nothing with them but the common noise and the general distraction, isolates a man in the worst way, separates him from reality in a way that is almost painless. It divides him off and separates him from other men and from his true self."[46]

He admitted that a monastery could be a City, and he was sure that a City could contain Communities. Even in his most bitter attacks upon the City he always admitted that all cities are not bad, that a city is really the people in it, and that if the people are sane the city will be sane. While cities are not naturally propitious places in which to worship God, he said, one can pray and love and be close to God in them, and if enough people in a given city should live the responsible contemplative life, the City will become the Community.[47] He explained: "Even where war has not yet touched, cities are in devastation and nonentity; and yet, once again, under the surface of glitter and trash, in the midst of all the mess of traffic, there are the people—sick and distraught, drunk, mad, melancholy, anguished or simply bored to extinction. It is the people that I love, not the holes in the City and not the glitter of business and of progress."[48] Merton did love the people and sought to make them aware of the temporal nature of their City and to call them to create a Community. He wrote on the problems of the City and tried to call its citizens' attention to the hope that lies in God and in working with God for the City's salvation.

But most significant of all, he encouraged those already in contemplative pursuits, both monastic and secular, to take the message of the Community to the City. He converted the Lucan Christmas story into an allegory to describe the relationship that should exist between the true Community, those who practice contemplation, and the City of which they are not yet a part. Because the City, or the Inn, had no room for Christ and did not even know of his impending birth, God chose to tell the good news first to the shepherds, whom Merton identified as the "remnant of the desert-dwellers, the nomads, the true Israel," or the contemplatives of a society.[49] They were given the responsibility of relating the news of Christ's birth to the City because they alone were receptive to the news; likewise, since the modern City is also unprepared for God's message, those who are separated from the City's ambitions and values will be given the message to relate to the world. Because the City can receive the message of hope only through the work of the Community, the Community is the City's only hope. Merton's social concern grew out of his awareness that as a member of the Community he must tell the story of God's love to the City with a social as well as spiritual interpretation.

Merton pictured the contemplative in society, whether a monk or a layman, as a Berenger. In Ionesco's play from the Theater of the Absurd, the character Berenger refuses to set aside his humanity and become a rhinoceros as everyone else has done, and while his refusal to "join the herd" keeps mankind from forgetting what true manhood is, he is branded a traitor to the race. Merton called the sickness that is so evident in those who have lost their sense of solitude and contemplation "rhinoceritis," and he said that most men living in modern cities suffer from this disease, which is marked by an inability to dissent from the rush of the herd. He called for more Berengers to face up to the uselessness of the City's values and renounce the collective mind so that they can find truth and reality. These Berengers, whether in a monastery or in a factory, would continually remind men of their true capacity for humanity and friendship, but they would run the risk of being labeled traitors.[50]

The contemplative in society, symbolized by Berenger, would always preserve his sense of solitude without renouncing his relationship with his fellowman; in fact, being no longer entranced by marginal concerns, he would be truly united with other men. He would renounce "the superficial imagery and the trite symbolism that pretend to make the relationship more genuine" and accept the responsibility of achieving the true relationship which should exist between men.[51] If enough men would accept the responsibilities of the contemplative life, Merton believed, the City could become the Community. The City that is the world could become the World Community, and the City that is America could become the American Community.

Because of his interest in bringing the Community's insights to bear upon world problems, Merton was intrigued by the writings of Karl Rahner, who has said that the church faces a diaspora situation in the latter half of the twentieth century. According to Rahner's theory, the hierarchy of the church will, in the near future, lose its power and the laity will have to do the church's work in the world. In the diaspora, or the scattering, the church's survival will depend not upon a massive ecclesiastical assault upon the world organized along military lines, as in the past, but upon "the openness, the freedom, the total sincerity with which the ordinary Christian" meets and challenges the non-Christian with the gospel in his own language. Rahner sees the diaspora not as a grim era to be borne bravely and stoically but as a challenge and promise of hope to the courageous Christian. The church, stripped of financial support from secular sources, will have to depend upon its ordinary members for survival, and even her missionary program will assume a new form: "the purity of individual witness."[52]

As a monk whose monastery would have to face such an eventuality, Merton said, "I am for the diaspora. I prefer it to the closed Medieval hegemony. It may offer much better chances of a real Christian life and brotherhood."[53] He did not mourn the old ecclesiastical system whose plaster cracked and split in the Reformation, whose roof fell in during the French Revolution, and whose walls collapsed in World War I. Modern man, he said, should rebuild the church, perhaps in a new style. He felt that the monastic orders, because they were less dependent upon the institutional church and the outside world, would survive the diaspora situation better than the rest of the church, and he felt that the monasteries would be purified by a period of time that required monks to be true servants of God rather than just organization men.[54]

He took issue with the conservative churchmen who rejected Rahner's thesis and blithely continued to teach that the Christian in the modern world should simply try to restore the power and prestige of medieval Christianity. Merton saw no hope of returning to the days when the church ruled society, and he seemed to feel that such a reversal of the present trend toward diaspora would be harmful to the church and to society. He thought that the church could best be the Bride of Christ when it was totally disestablished, and he warned the conservatives to abandon their philosophy of "Triumphalism" for the true hope, "not in Catholic power but in the eschatological victory of Christ."[55]

Although he was criticized for his liberalism, Merton called for reforms in the monastic orders so that the monasteries would be prepared for the diaspora. He explained that monasticism, which basically follows a pattern of organization established in an earlier historical period and implicitly supports political monarchy and temporal power for the church, must offer more than an energetic and totally organized excursion into the pre-Napoleonic past if it is to survive the diaspora. Monasteries must be more flexible, more capable of original and charismatic initiatives, and monks must once and for all rid themselves of "the fears and narrowness that make them dread organizational breakdowns and upheavals more than the loss of monastic spirit." But he also warned that the reformation of monastic ideals and patterns must be done with care and that the good and valuable must not be thrown away with the anachronisms. The accidents need reforming, but the essences must be retained, and Merton urged that the new forms be created by men who are well grounded in the values of the old forms. The primary essence of monasticism, according to Merton, is contemplation, and this must be retained because a monk must be more than a teacher or cheesemaker. A monk without contemplation would be useless in the diaspora.[56]

Merton believed that the exiled Russian monks who are now living in Paris may be the prototypes of the monk of the future. Expelled from their land as well as from their monasteries, they practice a "monasticism of the heart"; they are already in the diaspora. Following this pattern, the monk of the diaspora would be "the charismatic man of God, distinguished from the world only by his humility and his dedication, by his fidelity to life and to truth, rather than by his garments, the cloister in which he lives, by his hieratic gestures and ascetic practices."[57]

While Merton's diaspora monk would spend as much time, if not more, in solitary contemplation than is now the case, he would be more open to the world than he is today. On the one hand, he would be more like the desert fathers, more separated from the world, more radical in his rejection of society than ever before; on the other hand, he would search for truth outside the monastery more than ever before, seeking to communicate with others and come to the aid of the society outside the enclosure walls. He would first genuinely renounce the world and give himself fully to solitude, poverty, and prayer, and then he would open himself to his fellowman in the world. "The monk retains his own perspective and his own horizons which are those of the desert and of exile. But this in itself should enable him to have a special understanding of his fellow man in an age of alienation."[58]

Merton welcomed the diaspora because he felt that Christians would then become real Christians, non-Christians would then become real non-Christians, and monks would then become real monks. In the diaspora through a genuine renunciation of the world, an authentic solitude, and a serious life of prayer, the monk could prepare himself for fruitful communication with the world. Only when he and the atheist-intellectual, for example, attained a sense of complete polarity, understanding exactly who the other was, could they discover their brotherhood in sharing such common concerns as racial justice, world peace, or anything that concerns the well-being of mankind. Merton explained: "This dialogue will remain, in the life of the monk, a secondary and accidental concern. The monastery will by no means be organized *for* this as for an end, even though secondary, since the monastic charism is not 'for' anything else. It is what it is: the search for God in unconditional renunciation. Yet it paradoxically liberates the monk so that he can, when occasion exceptionally demands, communicate with his fellow man and indeed do much to 'give full scope to the forces of redemption' (Rahner) that must shape the world of his time."[59]

Merton's monastic ideal was a life of complete liberty from "the world" in the bad sense of the word, and even from the more "worldly" side of the church, and total freedom to contemplate God and his word. The monk should, from the point of view of his poverty, labor, solitude, and insecurity, gain an "understanding of the needs and sufferings of the men of his time" and be able to "enter into dialogue with those who are not monks and not even Christians."[60]

Merton's own life illustrated the diaspora monk's passion for communication as he met and corresponded with men of all intellectual persuasions while retiring ever more to a Trappist hermitage. He particularly courted the intellectuals, many of whom were antagonistic to his church and its traditions. Although he was considered something of an intellectual himself, especially before his conversion to Catholicism, it seemed odd to some Christians that a man involved in what might be thought of as an irrational vocation could communicate with and make such a favorable impression upon the intellectual community. But Merton felt that monks and intellectuals actually had a good deal in common because of their general distaste for modern society's sham, and he made a concerted effort to speak to them, believing that his withdrawal and contemplation made the task easier. He believed that by their rejection and criticism of the Establishment, modern intellectuals had in many ways assumed the burden which monks had carried in the Middle Ages, and he advised his fellow monks to observe them and follow their example of remaining free from the world and insipid goals.[61] He explained: "We need to form monks of the twentieth century who are capable of embracing in their contemplative awareness not only the theological dimensions of the mystery of Christ but also the possibilities of new understanding offered by non-Christian traditions and by the modern world of science and revolution."[62]

Perhaps this attitude helps to explain Merton's phenomenal popularity in secular America. A solitary contemplative, he was read and admired by urbanites; a recluse, he was respected and sometimes even adored by the young and socially militant. Although he withdrew from the city and from the active arena of social reform, he discovered a love for the city and the society in the depth of his contemplation, and when the occasion demanded that he address these areas he performed his task willingly and eloquently. It is of course possible that his popularity lay partly in the novelty of his position, in the fact that a city boy had gone to live in the woods and a young liberal had given up society, but it is more likely that he gained the attention of the American people because they realized that he was genuine: a monk who un-ashamedly rejected society's values and yet loved its people. Because he was authentic he was able to call many people back to the contemplation that had been so nearly lost in the modern world. His words after receiving an award of merit from the Catholic organization Pax express the philosophy of life which made his voice so prominent and influential: "A monastery is not a snail's shell, nor is religious faith a kind of spiritual fallout shelter into which one can plunge to escape the criminal realities of an apocalyptic age." Merton faced his world in the 1960s, and although his perspective was an abbey window his comments, criticism, and tentative answers ring with the authenticity that only great intelligence and honest concern can create.

Chapter Four

The Battle of Gog
and Magog

Although Thomas Merton became a monk to escape a world he had come to hate, he was never able to forget about it completely, and over the twenty-seven years of his monastic career his attraction to it took the form of an uncertain love affair, with all the attendant quarrels and emotional reconciliations. He said in 1941 that he never wanted to see the world again, but by the late 1950s he was again on speaking terms with it, and by the mid-1960s he was its friend and lover. When in 1965 his abbot finally permitted him to leave the monastery and take up residence in his long-desired hermitage, he vowed never again to discuss contemporary social problems and promised to write only on spiritual topics, but within weeks he discovered that he could not divorce himself from the world, and during those last three solitary years of his life he wrote some of his most impressive social commentaries.

Just a year before his death, in one of his rather common moments of self-analysis, Merton declared himself to be nonconformist, anti-modern, and isolated from the world and even the church, living too far off the main highway to jump onto every new bandwagon that passed.[1] This self-estimate is a bit harsh, as anyone who has read his more recent works can attest, for in the 1960s Merton understood the world and its problems surprisingly well for a monk, and in some ways his social criticism surpassed in quality and value many writers, especially other churchmen, who prided themselves on being deeply involved in worldly affairs. It is true that he was just as critical of the world in 1968 as he had been in 1941, finding very little in it that was lovely and speaking out time and again against its injustice and madness, but in 1968 his love for the world's people had deepened, and as a result his criticism contained positive suggestions for redemption, or at least improvement. When he opened his eyes again and looked upon the world he had left behind, he was able to see certain movements and events more clearly than many of his contemporaries who had watched them develop firsthand, and his comments on these movements and events which stood out in such bold relief for him are extremely enlightening. Merton's own personality, his ten-year absence from the world, and the peculiar perspective of a Trappist monastery's window combined to make his comments about the modern world fascinating. The clarity and accuracy of his analyses and conclusions make them worth heeding.

One problem of modern society with which Merton dealt at length was the cold war, the ideological, national, and military struggle between the Communist and free worlds which has threatened the security of the world since the Second World War. Karl Marx and his communist ideology had, by the mid-1950s, captured the imagination or the souls of half the world's population and seemed destined to gain even more, and Merton, himself a half-hearted Communist for a short time while a student at Columbia, criticized and evaluated communism at great length in books, articles, and poems. Although he felt that Marx himself was mentally ill and also a hopeless cynic, he called him a true genius who possessed perhaps the most perceptive mind of modern times. He agreed with Marx's contention that modern man's most dangerous and infectious disease is his slavery to money and machines, and he applauded Marx's keen analysis of the inconsistencies and contradictions of modern social institutions.[2] He particularly approved of Marx's denunciation of nineteenth-century liberalism which Merton described as the flaccid humanitarianism of bourgeois paternalism, a pious doctrine which permitted its adherents to evade the realities of social justice.[3]

But while Merton approved Marx's analysis of modern society's problems, he completely rejected Marx's solution to these problems. He pictured Marx as a neurotic whose bourgeois, Jewish conscience, struggling with a guilt which arose from the sight of so much social injustice, envisioned a classless society of perfectly honest workers led to victory by a perfectly honest Marx. Merton said that Marx's impossible dream, when actually applied to or forced upon a society, proved to be a nightmare: "Because Marx raged at himself and everyone else and wore out a path in his carpet walking up and down the room cursing his boils, there are now twenty million persons in Soviet forced labor camps."[4]

Merton also rejected Marx's conclusions about religion. He did not argue with Marx about the demonic nature of opiate religion, for he himself condemned religion when it is used as a smoke screen to veil economic problems, especially when it discourages men from solving their own problems by misusing the doctrine of the Will of God. But he rejected Marx's definition of religion and God, saying that Marx was not describing true Christianity or the real God. Instead of defining God as the Father of Jesus Christ who loved the world and its citizens, Marx accepted the definition of God being taught by the Establishment which he so despised and proceeded to condemn that abstract essence which had been built up to support an evil economy. Claiming that religion is a yoke to bind mankind to an unjust social order, Marx said that humanism must be atheistic, but Merton held that true Christianity is a movement to liberate men from such bondage.[5]

Merton agreed with a number of Marx's ideas and even seemed to understand the reasons for many of his errors, but he had little respect for the teachings and actions of Marx's successors in the Communist movement. He differed with Marx about many things, but he felt that Marx was a true humanist, something which he could not say for the Marxists. He felt that the Marxists had wandered so far away from Marx's original ideals that they had contradicted most of his teachings and had themselves become the demons which Marx condemned. These latter-day Communist saviors had abandoned Marx's call for economic honesty, he said, and had erected instead the greatest monument of lies and hypocrisy in all of history, paying lip service to Marx's condemnation of inconsistency and alienation while themselves increasing man's misery and intensifying his despair. By forcing their economic system and atheism upon other men they had clearly demonstrated to Merton the weakness of Marxist theory; far from liberating men they had brought about complete spiritual alienation.[6] Merton believed that Boris Pasternak, in his novel *Doctor Zhivago*, provided the most accurate critique of Marxism when he pointed out the foolishness of seeking immortality in a stone, which has already been stamped lifeless and dead. Instead of opening the door to the future, Merton said, Marxism had actually regressed into the ancient past, to the time of slavery before the coming of Christ.[7]

For Merton, then, Marx was a genius whose few severe blind spots have permitted his followers to justify slavery in the name of liberation, thus rendering Marx a false prophet. His attitude toward Marx is most clearly expressed in a long poem in which he describes Marx the Prophet running for his life, pursued by a wild dog. An omniscient narrator discusses the prophet's dilemma:

Oh prophet, when it was afternoon you told us:
"Tonight is the millenium,
The withering-away of the state.
The skies, in smiles, shall fold upon the world,
Melting all injustice in the rigors of their breezy love."
And all night long we waited at the desert's edge,
Hearing this wild-dog, only, on the far mountain,
Watching the white moon giggle in the stream!

Oh prophet, when it was night you came and told us:
"Tomorrow is the millenium,
The golden age!
The human race will wake up
And find dollars growing out of the palms of their hands,
And the whole world will die of brotherly love
Because the factories jig like drums
And furnaces feed themselves,
And all men lie in idleness upon the quilted pastures,
Turning their friendly radios and dreaming in the sun!"

But when the grey day dawned
What flame flared in the jaws of the avenging mills!
We heard the clash of hell within the gates of the embattled Factory
And thousands died in the teeth of those sarcastic fires!

And now the rivers are poisoned,
The skies rain blood
And all the springs are brackish with the taste
Of these your prophecies.
Oh prophet, tell us plainly, at last:
When is the day of our success?[8]

Because of the religious nature of Marxism and its vehement rejection of Christianity, Merton dealt in some detail with the relationship between communism and Christianity. He believed that Marxism as a philosophy had had a positive effect upon the church, modifying its attitude toward history and consequently toward this present world. Before Hegelian Marxism, Merton said, Catholicism had for centuries operated under a Carolingian world view in which the condemned world, for the most part unaware of the redemptive power of the crucifixion, and the redeemed church were seen to be waiting for the end of time when all men would acknowledge the Lordship of Christ; in the meantime, the church had a duty to impose Christian morals upon the unregenerate society so as to save it from God's wrath. Marxism, by proclaiming a new era of goodness within time itself, had caused many Catholic thinkers to reinterpret this world view and overcome the more unproductive elements of their otherworldliness. For this effect Merton was grateful, and he illustrated his point by showing Marx's positive influence upon a man like Teilhard de Chardin, who had abandoned the concept of a God enthroned "out there" for a God who is "absolute future," who will manifest himself in and through man "by the transformation of man and the world through science oriented to Christ."[9]

Merton held that Christianity and the ideal of communism are not necessarily antagonistic, although Christianity and the Communist movement are indeed enemies. True communism, true sharing of goods, is in fact best exemplified by the Cistercian monastic order within the Catholic church. He explained: "The Cistercians have carried communism to its ultimate limit. They not only hold their farm and monastery and all the things in it as common property, not one having a legitimate personal claim to anything so small as a handkerchief or a pin or a piece of paper, but they share all their failings and all their weaknesses and all their sicknesses of soul and body."[10] Besides, Merton argued, a Christian cannot hate anyone, not even a Communist, for his faith is based upon a God of mercy and love. The mark of a Christian, he said, is love for mankind, and while he may disagree with a Communist he must love him.[11] For Merton, the anti-Communist Christian crusader is worse than a pathetic Don Quixote; he is basically unchristian.

Christianity is opposed to all mass movements, Merton stated, for they are intrinsically detrimental to man's well-being. He explained that the founders of totalitarian states, who are leaders of mass movements, put their trust in money and technology rather than in God to build a better world and thereby succeed only in creating a monolithic society which suppresses the creativity of its citizens. The Communists, being leaders and founders of a mass movement which has become totalitarian, have indeed increased production while subjecting men to some of history's most monstrous indignities.[12]

Merton pointed out that the death of Jesus is the most obvious example of Christianity's opposition to mass movements such as communism. Because the mass movement mentality sees a man not as a real person but as part of a group, it snuffs out the individuals in its midst, labeling them enemies. Jesus was mistaken for the enemy and was killed because he did not conform to the pattern of behavior dictated by the dominant group of his day. Thus, Merton reasoned, the Christian, who builds his faith upon the example of Jesus, must oppose the intolerance, prejudice, and hatred of those with crippled minds who cannot love another person as an individual; he must seek to restore to all men the capacity to love, which is the true image of God in man.[13] According to Merton, a Christian's duty is to "preserve the human person in his integrity, his freedom and his individuality, and to arm him spiritually against the peril of totalitarianism."[14]

Merton took issue with those who say that the Christian ideal of the kingdom of God is in reality a mass movement. He saw it instead as the "Kingdom of One who being equal to God took the form of a servant and suffered," and he believed that in the kingdom of God the higher members exist and work for the lower, while a mass movement is a pyramid on which a few strong men climb to the summit and live sumptuously on the "labors of the huge anonymous mass which sacrifices itself in adoration of them."[15] He had to admit, however, that the church, which should be a mystical body, has in the past and could in the future, become a mass movement and a totalitarian organization, when its basic teachings are perverted by turning from the example of Christ's self-sacrifice. Even the church has and can become a mob in which the individual loses his identity and responsibility when Christianity is reduced to a set of slogans to defend, but when this happens it is no longer the true church. Merton gave as examples of such perversion the sacking of Constantinople by the crusaders, the destruction of Indian Central America by the Christian Conquistidores, and the more recent call of some Christians to wipe out the "Red Menace" with a nuclear bomb. He warned: "It is all too easy for us to lose sight of Christ and His charity, and to exchange the basic truths of the Gospel for new slogans that promise to be 'more effective' in rallying thousands to our cause. Let us beware. The blaring of loud-speakers, the roaring of slogans, the tramp of marching thousands, will never produce anything but alienated fanatics."[16] Merton said that the Christian must oppose mass movements such as communism. For Merton, a Christian's ultimate loyalty must be to Christ and his example of sacrifice. But again he emphasized that Christianity and communism are ideological, not physical enemies. The Christian may battle the Communist with words but not with guns, for the Christian's most precious gift is love, the ability to love one's enemies.[17]

Merton obviously did not approve of communism as it has been realized in Russia and China, but he was also critical of the free world's alternative to communism, a philosophy which he sometimes called Americanism. Although he was himself an American, he was skeptical of American democracy when it becomes Americanism just as he was skeptical of the ideal of communism when it becomes the Communist movement. He saw both of these philosophies as threats to Christianity and, more importantly, to man's freedom. Merton saw developing, along with a militant totalitarian communism, a militant Americanism, a blighted philosophy whose vicious flame is fed by what Merton called the American myth: the myth of America the Earthly Paradise. He acknowledged that a national myth is necessary and even good for a people, for it helps them to create the conditions which their myth describes. But he also believed that America's myth, once a positive aid to this country's development, had become a daydream, perhaps even an evasion, and certainly a negative factor in America's growth.

America was indeed the Earthly Paradise to the early settlers, Merton explained, a land without history and therefore without sin. Those early settlers were escaping a historical Europe grown old in wickedness, escaping history's burden of sin. They were returning to life's source, starting life anew in a land without original sin, a Paradise. Merton explained that for four hundred years the frontier existed, permitting Americans continuously to leave areas that were being corrupted to find a new place with no history and thus no sin. Even the South, despite its slavery, was thought to be a Paradise until the brutal national trauma of the Civil War brought its myth into the light of open scrutiny and squashed it under heel. Soon after the close of the Civil War the western frontier closed, and Americans had no more Paradise, being hemmed in as they were by their sin of enslaving the Negro and killing the Indian. Since the destruction of the feudal South and the closing of the western frontier, the myth of America the Earthly Paradise has been dead, but some Americans will not give it up to burial, making of it an evasion of responsibility.

Merton said that it was the desire to keep this myth alive that caused Americans to ride to the rescue of the underdog in the Cuban Revolution, World War I, and World War II, always defeating the Outlaw with frontier zeal. He said that cowboy shows are popular today because Americans still enjoy seeing themselves as straight-shooting, hard-hitting, clean-living frontiersmen, inhabiting a Paradise without sin. For a time, he said, the rest of the world believed the myth because of our successes, but in recent days they have begun to see that we have plenty of history and little Paradise, and now the cry "Yankee go home" includes the cruel implication that home is no longer the perfect place for the Yankee to be. It is now foolish for Americans to preach to the poorer nations the wisdom of adopting our way of life because everyone now knows that "we are in the same mess as all the rest of them." He said that the honest American cannot even guard his myth by staying home and watching himself wearing a white hat on television, for the news media constantly interrupt the cowboy shows with bulletins showing blacks protesting the injustices of American society. The myth of America the Earthly Paradise has been exploded both from within and from without, Merton concluded, and Americans must move forward to create a new and better history rather than try to return to a time of no history at all.[18]

Merton opposed Americanism as thoroughly as he opposed communism. When he went outside the monastery in the 1950s, he found an America clinging to a dead myth in spite of the real problems of the world and believing itself to be perfectly honest and peaceloving while its enemy, the Devil's army, sought to storm the gates of Paradise. And he saw the Communists abandoning their leader's call for international peace and social reform and simply adding to modern man's alienation from himself and God.

And so he opposed both great powers, especially since they had locked themselves into a cold war which threatened the future of man.

Merton's most explicit response to the struggle between the United States and Russia, which he discovered upon emerging from his self-imposed exile, may be found in his "Letter to Pablo Antonio Cuadra Concerning Giants."[19] Using characterizations suggested to him by the French existentialist Albert Camus,[20] Merton said that the two great powers are like sorcerer's apprentices, spending billions of dollars on space exploration and nuclear weapons while failing to feed, clothe, and shelter two-thirds of the human race. They are like the twins Gog and Magog in the book of Ezekiel, he said, each with great power and little sanity, each telling lies with great conviction. Gog, or the East, is a lover of power while Magog, or the West, is a lover of money; their idols differ in appearance, and they stand opposite each other, but their insanity is the same; they are the two faces of Janus. Both claim to be humanistic, he said, yet they care only about names, slogans, and labels. If a citizen is not properly classified, Gog shoots him, while Magog deprives him of a home, a job, or a seat on the bus. In both lands "life and death depend on everything except what you *are*."[21]

Merton lived in Magog's land, and although he and Magog seldom agreed on ethical questions he conceded that Magog at least let him live in peace, which Gog would probably not have done. He admitted that Magog was not overly demanding, permitting his citizens to disagree and asking only for lip service while pressuring them to conform, and he even half trusted the strain of idealism which lay at the base of Magog's nature, feeling that it was a sign that Magog was still a bit human under all his materialism. But he feared that Magog's ideals, which were out in the open for everyone to see, gravely handicapped him in his cold war struggle with Gog and that one day he might set aside those ideals in order to win the war.

Magog is a Christian, but Merton described his Christianity as one of money, action, passive crowds, parades, and loudspeakers. He said that Magog, who in reality has no faith, is cynically tolerant of the sentimental, athletic Christ promoted by Christian artists because such a Christ is useful to Magog in his fight with Gog. This Christ protests against atheistic Gog, not against the money changers in the temple, and he supports Magog in all his undertakings. Magog, by tolerating this useful Christ, appears to be quite religious, but Merton pointed to the hypocrisy of his actions.

Merton described Gog and Magog as two giant insects with societies something like anthills, "without purpose, without meaning, and without spirit and joy." He predicted that the two hills would eventually destroy each other and that the Southern Hemisphere would inherit the earth. India, Arabia, Africa, Latin America, Australia, and Indonesia would become the leaders of the world. While Merton certainly did not look forward to a nuclear war that would destroy the Northern Hemisphere, he did say that the world would be better off if it were led by these southern peoples with their different outlook on life. He believed that their philosophy of life, which he said is more concrete than abstract, more hieratic than pragmatic, "intuitive and affective rather than rationalistic and aggressive," would create a much better world than now exists. He advised the surviving "Third World," the society that would perhaps live through the bomb, to "be unlike the giants Gog and Magog. Mark what they do, and act differently. Mark their official pronouncements, their ideologies, and without any difficulty you will find them hollow. Mark their behavior, their bluster, their violence, their blandishments, their hypocrisy: by their fruits you shall know them."[22]

Merton called both Gog and Magog sinners because of their neglect of the poor, being so obsessed with the cold war that they forgot the very people they claimed to serve. The United States with its money and machines promised to "abolish poverty all over the world," and Russia with its revolution and machines promised to "abolish poverty all over the face of the earth," but while they were making their promises poverty grew worse and had actually become "destitution, misery, starvation and outright slavery." Merton ridiculed Gog and Magog for playing their little cold war games while most of the world remained poor, not poor in the "somewhat dignified and natural poverty of a primitive culture," but slum poor.[23]

Merton placed the blame for the modern world's widespread poverty upon the two superpowers who have destroyed primitive cultures without replacing them with any higher civilization. Taking men away from jobs and villages that were poor but primitively beautiful, they have forced men into city slums where they lose all meaning in life and eventually starve to death. He said that if such displaced persons in Magog's land become dissatisfied with their lot and make themselves too conspicuous, spoiling rich men's appetites, they are thrown into concentration camps called ghettos; if their counterparts in Gog's land complain, they are put into work gangs, fed with slogans, and shot if they protest further. Magog keeps his poor out of sight, pretending they are not there, while Gog keeps his poor moving continually, pretending that something positive is being accomplished. Both Gog and Magog, Merton said, refuse to see that the vast majority of the world's population have no beds, food, shoes, education, or medical care; both of them salve their consciences with the idea that poverty is being taken care of by some agency or bureau which has actually washed its hands of the whole affair.[24]

One of Merton's most impressive translations was the diary of a simple Italian priest, Don Primo Mazzolari, who it seems said what Merton wished to say to Gog and Magog. In the introduction to the translation, Merton expressed his shame at being a part of today's world and proclaimed that he had no faith at all in the plans being made to solve the problems of the poor of all nations. An excerpt from Merton's translation underlines his own feelings about the cold war and the poor, who are its saddest victims. He quoted Primo: "Between the poor and God there is a close resemblance, a continuous encounter. Didn't Jesus say we would be judged by the way in which we had, or had not, fed, refreshed and comforted Him under the guise of the poor man? No poor man, no Jesus. The poor being there, and God being there: it is the same. Makes us uncomfortable. Better if God wasn't there. Better if the poor weren't there."[25]

Although Merton agreed with many of the original intentions and goals of both communism and American idealism, he opposed the Communist movement and Americanism, calling them perversions of their original images. He felt that both had abandoned the morality required to achieve their initial purposes and had thus forfeited their rights to the allegiance of the people. He explained that while communism long ago surrendered its ideals and became a totalitarian dictatorship, mimicking the hated Nazi enemy, America was close to doing the same thing. In his more pessimistic moments he even said that America might well become a fascist state, liquidate its people and "inferior" races, and engage the Communist bloc in a cataclysmic nuclear war.

In March 1968 Merton said that America then reminded him of the Germany which he had visited in 1932, just before the establishment of Hitler's Nazi regime. He recalled the hatred of the Jews, the desire for international prestige that would lead to world war, and the irresponsible refusal of most German citizens to oppose the approaching evil of Nazism. He felt that all these impending signs of doom were present in America during that election year: expressions of hatred toward the rebelling Negro; the desire to retain an image as the country which has never lost a war by moving ever closer to a major land war in Asia; and a callous attitude on the part of most Americans toward the task of opposing political candidates who might well, according to Merton, establish a fascist state and stumble into a nuclear war. Because these fears were not immediately realized some might be tempted to minimize their dangers, but the attitudes and potentials still exist, and many other voices have joined Merton's warnings since his death.

Merton opposed the cold war between East and West primarily because he feared that an escalation into a nuclear confrontation might destroy the world. He explained that while men of the nineteenth century thought wars were coming to an end men in the 1960s had come to see that the fire of war dies down only to spring up again higher than before. He felt that the smouldering flame was preparing to leap up again and destroy mankind, for the bomb which ended the war against Japan had started an arms race that could end in catastrophe. Merton pictured modern man entering the post-Christian era with a vengeance, gripped by a war madness, plunging headlong into war even while saying he is attempting to preserve the peace.[26] He warned that with both the United States and Russia prepared to use nuclear weapons for defense, for first-strike attack, and even for retaliation after one had already been destroyed, a nuclear war was quite likely to occur, perhaps by accident. In such an event, he believed, whole civilizations would be destroyed indiscriminately, and perhaps the whole human race would be lost forever.[27]

Most of Merton's statements concerning the dangers of nuclear war were made in the early 1960s before the Test Ban Treaty of 1963, and they consequently were prophetic calls for men to return to good sense and Christian reason. Some of them sound a bit dated today, but while the complexion of this problem has been slightly altered, the danger of nuclear war is still imminent, and Merton's warnings and suggestions are not at all irrelevant for the contemporary scene. They clearly demonstrate the moral fervor, sagacity, and limitations of Merton the Christian pacifist as social analyst. He called the cold war a "political dance of death" which was bringing mankind step by step closer to the brink of destruction, and he warned that the babel of voices suggesting solutions to the problem in his day was just confusing the issues. Some were advocating a first-strike attack on the enemy's key cities and military installations in order to prevent war while others were advocating only a second-strike attack, massive retaliation on the enemy's cities if we should be attacked first. A few "optimists" were even arguing that a limited war, using conventional weapons or tactical nuclear weapons, would be a positive good, for it would prevent an all-out nuclear confrontation. Merton scorned all these solutions, but especially did he reject the solution of the so-called realists who were calculating "acceptable losses" and looking forward to the time when survivors would crawl out of their shelters and resume business as usual.[28]

Merton said that there was no effective control over the use of nuclear weapons. The United Nations had proved itself incapable of influencing the crucial decisions of the great nations. He felt that because the powerful nations, those with nuclear stockpiles, use the United Nations as a wrestling arena but ignore it when their interests are involved, a nuclear war could break out whenever a belligerent felt strong enough. He warned that this "balance of terror" could not last much longer: "The slightest false move, the most innocent miscalculation, an ill chosen word, a misprint, a trivial failure in the mechanism of a computer, and one hunderd million people evaporate, burn to death, go up in radioactive dust, or crawl about the face of the earth waiting for death to release them from agony."[29]

He feared that the huge stockpiles of nuclear weapons, the stalemate in the cold war, and the moral uncertainty of the latter half of the twentieth century were driving men to extreme positions. Some were surrendering to passive despair while others were giving in to fanaticism; the first accepted the absurdity of the situation and adopted a "drugged existence which renounces all effort and all hope," and the fanatic called for a nuclear showdown to end the uncertainty and anticipation. Merton warned that both types, by their very different actions, could contribute to that nuclear showdown.[30] He believed that the presence of such a destructive power, the moral paralysis of world leaders, and the confusion and passivity of the masses on both sides of the iron curtain created the greatest crisis in human history.[31]

Merton felt that the cold war was creating an atmosphere in which the great powers could easily commit national suicide. The world had been poised on the brink of nuclear war so long that its citizens in the event of a small attack, or even the mere rumor of an attack, might turn on each other in a selfish attempt to survive, and he said that suicide on a national scale would be even worse than on the individual level.[32]

He also blamed the cold war for America's and Russia's neglect of the emerging nations' economic and spiritual needs. America, once seen by backward nations as the true defender of liberty, justice, and peace, the hope for a better future, was now seen as a power-mad monster. The typical cold war personality characterized by anger, ignorance, and frustration had asserted itself in America, making her forfeit her position as the inspiration and friend of underdeveloped nations, causing her to act more like atheistic Russia than like her Christian forebears. The cold war, which he knew could lead to nuclear war, was to his dismay being fought by two powers who possessed great potential for destruction with little moral direction.[33]

Merton was one of the first theologians to see that the cold war threat of nuclear war and destruction had created a new ethic, warping traditional Christian ethics for its own needs. Some clergymen, he observed, had even begun to defend nuclear war as a moral act, and he felt that this "slow corruption of the Christian ethical sense" was the result of the weakening of human compassion under stress, of theorizing in a vacuum, and of "juggling with moral clichés devoid of serious content." He said that the only reason Americans could join in the cold war dance of death, asking God to "justify the moral blindness and hybris of generals and industrialists, and to bless nuclear war as a holy and apocalyptic crusade" was that they had completely abandoned Christian ethics.[34] Christian ideals had been so totally disregarded that those Christians who spoke out clearly against nuclear war were branded as Communist sympathizers by Christians and non-Christians alike.

He believed that only when Christian ethics are perverted can Christians long for a destructive war that will eliminate their enemy.[35]

Merton wondered why more peace demonstrations like the ones before World War II were not being carried out against nuclear weapons. Although a small number of Quakers and Mennonites had protested, most Protestant and Catholic thinkers spent their time trying to reconcile what they considered to be an inevitable nuclear war with the traditional Christian doctrine of just war. Merton warned that these men were twisting Christian ethics, and he called on Christian theologians to state unequivocally that "the massive and uninhibited use of nuclear weapons, either in attack or in retaliation, is contrary to Christian morality." He said bluntly that the Christian who would not publicly brand nuclear war as "immoral, inhuman and absurd" had abandoned traditional Christian moral theology.[36]

Merton took issue particularly with those Christian theologians who were saying that a nuclear war was not as dangerous to the world as a Communist takeover and that the Communists would close the church doors and precipitate an era of darkness unless they were repelled with the bomb. Merton scorned the idea that the destruction of nations, cities, and whole populations would be only physical evil while Communist domination would be moral evil. He said that this "fantastic piece of nonsense has no basis in logic, ethics, politics or sound moral theology," and he blamed the American mass media, which he said had constantly oversimplified the facts about the Communist threat, for creating an American mentality which had warped Christian ethics into such a demonic form.[37]

Merton theorized that the root of all wars is fear; men are afraid of themselves as well as their opponents. Men fight because they do not trust themselves, and they do not trust themselves because they do not trust God. For Merton it is not so much hatred of others as hatred of self that causes war; men are alarmed at their own evil but cannot consciously admit it, and so they project it upon others and seek to destroy that "enemy" who is carrying their own evil. He believed that each man or each nation creates its own scapegoat, a mythical and sinful enemy whose death will supposedly end all evil, strife, and war, and he asserted that only the man or nation that has learned to love by knowing God can success-fully "exorcise the fear which is at the root of all war."[38]

Merton believed that war is illegitimate because its source is man's inability to accept God's love, and he said that a nuclear war would be especially evil because of the enormous number of people who would be killed. Admitting that a Christian could legiti-mately hold that a limited nuclear war in self-defense is consistent with the doctrine of just war, he was further forced to concede that the strategic use of chemical, bacteriological, or nuclear weapons is theoretically permissible under stringent conditions. But he argued that when one comes face to face with the "absolutely real and imminent *probability* of massive and uncontrolled destruction" of a nuclear war, when one faces the probability of the annihilation of civilization and even of human life, one does not have the luxury of choice. He said that no one can morally choose to kill millions of people, most of them innocent bystanders. "Even though we may feel justified in risking the destruction of our own cities and those of the enemy, we have no right whatever to bring destruction upon helpless small nations which have no interest whatever in the war and ask only to survive in peace. It is not up to us to choose that they should be dead rather than red."[39] He pointed out that a nuclear war could not be limited to military targets, that an all-out nuclear war would mean "massive and indiscriminate destruction of targets" chosen not for their military significance but for their ability to terrify and annihilate whole populations, as was true in the case of Hiroshima, a city chosen for the atomic bomb because it had not been bombed before and could best demonstrate the bomb's destructive powers.

Merton warned Christians that a nuclear war would destroy Christianity, particularly if a "Christian" nation started and won the war. Quoting Saint Augustine's statement that the weapon which one uses to destroy an enemy passes through one's own heart before it reaches the enemy, Merton pointed out that if Christians should use nuclear weapons to destroy their ideological enemy they would destroy their own effective witness in the world. No one would ever again respect or be converted to Christianity, a religion whose adherents committed mass murder.[40] He complained that in the midst of this terrifying situation Christians were morally paralyzed, so hypnotized by the mass media, so bewildered by the silence of their religious leaders, and so aware of the failures of the pre-World War II peace movements that they had withdrawn into a passive fatalism. In Merton's words they were "immobile, inert, passive, tongue-tied, ready and even willing to succumb to the demons of the modern world."[41] He blamed the silence of the church on the fear of church leaders to take a stand and lead their people to stand up for justice and right. He accused Christian moralists of debating the issues so far in the background that they had no influence on America's nuclear policies, and he did not try to defend them against the charge of selling mankind down the river in order to maintain the status and social advantages which the church enjoys in the modern world.[42]

Merton called upon church leaders to speak out on the evil of nuclear warfare and thereby to inspire their laity to follow. In a review of *The Christian Failure,* the diary of Ignace Lepp, a French priest who almost single-handedly led clerical opposition to Nazi control over France during World War II, Merton called on other Christian spokesmen to join him in his crusade against nuclear war. Father Lepp had theorized that most of the French clergy submitted to Nazi control because their seminary training had not put them in touch with reality; they were prepared to face theological problems but unprepared to face social ones, and they failed to be true Christians in the moment of their nation's greatest crisis. Merton agreed with Father Lepp's condemnation of a theology that does not address itself to social problems; he said that the gravest threat to religion and to society in the modern age was the unwillingness of Christian leaders to protest social evil, injustice, and war; and he reminded the clergy that their primary task is to serve God rather than man.[43]

Just prior to the concluding session of Vatican II Merton wrote an open letter to the American Catholic hierarchy in which he discussed the decisions of the council. He said that the council's primary task was to proclaim the gospel of love and hope to modern man in his own language without distorting the message. Since this message is not bound to any specific culture or age, the council should free it from its medieval and baroque language without identifying it too closely or firmly with the present confused, technological society; it should make its eternal truths speak to current problems and questions. He pointed out that since the greatest current world problem is the threat of nuclear war the council should apply the eternal truth of love and peace to this problem and condemn nuclear war as immoral. The positive achievements of the earlier sessions would be neutralized, he argued, if the council failed to condemn the use of modern weapons and the pursuit of total nuclear war. The poor men all over the world, he believed, were looking to the church as the last hope of protection from militarists and power-mad politicians, and the church could not afford to plunge mankind into deeper despair by approving the social evils that oppress them. He concluded: "What matters is for the Bishops and the Council to bear witness clearly and without any confusion to the Church's belief in the power of love to save and transform not only individuals but society. Do we or do we not believe that love has this power? If we believe it, what point is there in using language of adroit compromise in order to leave the last word, in matters which affect the very survival of man, not to the Gospel but to power politics?"[44] The council, while making several statements about war, did not reach Merton's hopes or expectations.

Merton continually scolded churchmen for not speaking out against nuclear war when they possessed the revelation of God's love for the world. He warned that the church was in danger of missing its primary mission for this age, saving mankind from nuclear war, unless it awakened and took a stand. In his *Conjectures of a Guilty Bystander* he demonstrated the church's dilemma: "I am told by a high superior: 'It is not your place to write about nuclear war: that is for the bishops.' I am told by a moral theologian: 'How can you expect the bishops to commit themselves on the question of peace and war, unless they are advised by theologians?' Meanwhile the theologians sit around and preserve their reputations. Pretty soon they will no longer have any reputations to preserve."[45]

Merton was especially disturbed that none of the popes had formally condemned the use of nuclear weapons, and in various articles he tried to explain this neglect, apparently hoping to convince himself as well as his readers. For example, he once explained that the popes had not formally condemned the use of hydrogen bombs because to condemn a specific weapon would leave some verbal gymnasts free to make the pope appear to be approving other kinds of weapons.[46] Another time he explained that the popes had not condemned nuclear weapons because the weapons condemned themselves. Since their only purpose is to commit mass murder, he reasoned, and since the church has always opposed murder in all forms the popes had no reason to say what every thoughtful person already knew. The sin of nuclear war, he explained, is like the sin of adultery; neither sin has ever been condemned *ex cathedra* because they are both such obvious transgressions of God's laws that no pope has ever found it necessary to say the obvious.[47]

Still another time and place Merton argued that the popes' previous statements, their condemnation of certain aspects of war before the discovery of nuclear power, satisfied the need for a formal condemnation of nuclear war. He recalled Pius XII's declaration after the blitzkrieg of Poland in 1939 that the unlawful use of conventional weapons against refugees and civilians "cried out to heaven for vengeance," and he pointed out that in 1939 Pius also condemned all glorification of war as a deviation of the human heart and mind and that in 1954 Pius declared that from the moment it becomes so destructive that its effects cannot be controlled and limited to military uses a weapon is immoral.[48] He argued that it is in deference to the ancient Catholic doctrine of the right of self-defense that the popes had not specifically forbidden the use of nuclear weapons for defense in case of attack, but he also warned that the popes' reticence to condemn the use of nuclear weapons did not imply approval of a nuclear first-strike on an enemy's heartland or upon his cities; nor did it give approval to a first-strike on a military installation which is near a city.[49]

Using Pius XII's statement that a weapon is immoral when it becomes so destructive that it cannot be controlled, Merton claimed to have papal support for his sermons against the use of nuclear weapons. He believed that both Pius XII and John XXIII had said in so many words that the new means of warfare, especially nuclear weapons, have upset the traditional Catholic norms of morality, that they have created a new kind of war in which the concept of "just war" is irrelevant. Thus Merton said, "A war of total annihilation simply cannot be considered a 'just war,' no matter how good the cause for which it is undertaken."[50] But he was obviously bothered by the vagueness of the popes' statements about "uncontrollable" weapons. Pius had not said at what specific point a weapon passes beyond man's control; indeed, the argument could be made that nuclear weapons are controllable under the proper conditions. Merton warned against any lax interpretation of Pius's words, pointing out that a twenty megaton hydrogen bomb, when dropped on Leningrad or New York, would under no circumstances be under control. He interpreted what he believed Pius meant to say: "if there was uncontrolled annihilation of everybody in Leningrad, without any discrimination between combatants and non-combatants, enemies, friends, women, children, infants and old people, then the use of the bomb would be 'not lawful under any title' especially in view of the 'bonus' effects of fallout drifting over neutral territory, certainly without control."[51]

The world which Merton addressed in the 1960s was in deep trouble, its sky dark, its future uncertain. It was gripped by the icy blasts of a cold war which was destroying America's ideals, warping Christian morality, and moving the world ever closer to a nuclear disaster. Merton did not stop with a pessimistic analysis, however; he could not be content simply to curse the world that had come to such an impasse and a church that stood by morally paralyzed. He made a valiant attempt to offer solutions to the problems that were facing his world, and for the most part these solutions were pertinent and worthy of consideration.

Merton gave little thought to the personal consequences of his outspoken stand against war. He believed all war to be wrong, especially nuclear war, and he wrote many passionate statements of his position. He often clashed with other clergymen over social positions, one being an argument with a group of hawkish chaplains over the legitimacy of the war in Vietnam. Merton thought that the argument between those who advocated a strong nationalistic policy in Vietnam and those who, like himself, advocated peace was as crucial as the clash between "conservative churchmen and Galileo on the structure of the solar system," and he left no doubt that he thought of himself as one of the twentieth-century Galileos. He was so sure that he was right that he accused his opponents of refusing to listen to enlightened reasoning: "no moral argument has any weight with them because they are, without knowing it, obsessed and morally blind—just as the people who opposed and condemned Galileo were, in terms of the new physics, scientific illiterates."[52]

Although he received severe criticism for his part in the war protest, specifically for being a spiritual adviser to a young Kentuckian who rejected the military draft in 1968 and for being friends with the rebellious priests Daniel and Philip Berrigan, he never ceased to speak out clearly and precisely on the moral issue of the war. When he received the Pax medal for his writings on behalf of peace, he said that he was embarrassed to receive a prize for just doing his duty, the duty of any Christian. He concluded that it was like getting a medal for daily work, obeying traffic signs, or paying bills.

Although he addressed his remarks about war to all sensible men, he talked primarily to Christians who, because of their faith in God the Creator, should feel a natural sense of duty to preserve and protect God's creation, the earth and all its life, particularly its human life. And he felt that Christians, of all those who believe in God, were potentially the most effective opponents of nuclear war, for their faith is also based upon the doctrine that God became man in Jesus Christ and that this Christ loved the world enough to die for it. The Christian, he reasoned, should best be able to understand his duty to preserve the life of man whom God has sanctified.[53] He thus sought to awaken Christians to the truth that every man is Christ and that "human nature, identical in all men, was assumed by the logos in the Incarnation, and that Christ died out of love for all men, in order to live in all men. Consequently we have the obligation to treat every other man as Christ himself, respecting his life as if it were the life of Christ, his rights as if they were the rights of Christ."[54]

In his early writings on nuclear war Merton seemed to feel that any action against the use of nuclear weapons would be beneficial. In later statements, however, he singled out several approaches to the problem which, while not totally without merit, were certainly imperfect for the modern age.[55] One was conventional pacifism, which in its traditional form depends upon the conscience of the individual Christian and has no inherent social orientation. Since nuclear war is a problem that involves all human society, such conventional pacifism, with its individualistic orientation, would be not only inadequate but perhaps in certain circumstances harmful, Merton said.

Similar consequences would result from a simple call for unilateral disarmament. Merton declared that to ask America to destroy all her weapons in hopes that Russia would do likewise would be patently foolhearty, immature, and simplistic. Such an approach, he said, would actually make war all the more inevitable by making one country appear to be strong enough to attack another without fear of retaliation, and it would also strip away all vestiges of psychological security which American citizens have as a result of their store of nuclear deterrents. Such a suggestion would cast a bad light upon all attempts to achieve peace.

Also inadequate would be a purely spiritual witness against nuclear war, said the monk whose life was devoted to spiritual witness. As an older and wiser man he said that it was no longer adequate—because of the seriousness of the threat to man's future—simply to stand up and proclaim the world to be wicked, as he himself had done years before. In these dangerous days, he said, it is not enough to reject this world and call men away from it to repentance without sending them back into the world to help solve its problems. Christians, monks included, must get involved in the peace movement, not just withdraw and preach sermons.

Similarly it would be inadequate to teach the traditional Catholic doctrine of just war. Merton believed that this doctrine, which has always sanctioned war if it is defensive and if proper measures are taken to avoid pillage and the death of innocent people, was in its traditional form inadequate for the modern nuclear situation. Nuclear weapons had so altered the nature of war, bringing instant death to millions of noncombatants, that just war was no longer possible and might be simply an excuse to tolerate a nuclear exchange of fire. He did say, however, that just war in a reinterpreted sense might be helpful.

Merton was not content with simply pointing out the imperfections of these approaches to nuclear war; he offered concrete suggestions about the activities in which concerned Christians might engage. He believed that Christians must recapture the faith which has been nearly lost since the beginning of the cold war. He explained that so many Christians had developed a "cold war religion" by which they could glorify a nuclear war with Russia as a Christian crusade that the true Christian conscience had been eroded, if not permanently abandoned. This cold war religion "not only blinds us to true Christian values but makes all our judgments spring from this ground of sterility and frustration in which the weeds of hatred and incipient fascism (or Communism for that matter) very easily flourish."[56] Merton asked the Christian to stand back and regain his perspective instead of just repeating religious clichés. He encouraged him to cultivate an inner ground of faith and purity of conscience without which he could never hope to detach himself from selfish interests and peripheral concerns of his materially wealthy but spiritually dead society. While Christians must in every possible way defend the religious, political, and cultural values which give meaning to their lives, they must not defend them by advocating a war which would in effect destroy these values.[57]

Merton also called on the leaders of the church, the hierarchy as well as the theologians, to correct certain errors in their own thinking which had encouraged the cold war religion. He suggested that they correct their deviations from traditional Christian moral teachings and rethink many of these teachings in the light of present circumstances. On the other hand, they must return to the ancient principles of morality as revealed in the Gospels' ethic of love and nonviolence, which was accepted at least in principle during the Middle Ages but which he thought was being given only lip service in the 1960s. On the other hand, because nuclear weapons were so different from conventional weapons of the past they must rethink and reinterpret the ethic of love in terms of present needs. Merton believed that in an age when machines were doing most of the planning and actual fighting of wars, when wars might be fought in outer space, and when millions of people could be killed instantly, older interpretations of the never-dated Christian ethic of love might well be inadequate and perhaps even evil.[58]

One area of Christian social theology which Merton thought needed to be reinterpreted was the ethical philosophy of pacifism, which some few Christians had adopted as a way of life but which most had abandoned as old-fashioned and inadequate. Merton suggested that Christians in the twentieth century become relative pacifists, that they agree to participate in just war but not in nuclear war, which he believed could never be just. A relative pacifist would follow the traditional Catholic doctrine of just war except where nuclear weapons were involved. While the Gospels did not permit a Catholic to be an absolute pacifist, Merton believed that they did permit him to be a pacifist in certain circumstances, such as when he believes that even a limited, non-nuclear war is unjust or may escalate to an unjust size. Merton taught his readers that "the unrestricted use of nuclear weapons for the single purpose of annihilation of civilian centers is completely immoral. It is nothing but murder and is never permitted, any more than a nuclear preemptive strike on civilian centers would be permitted by Christian ethics."[59]

Merton grieved over the fact that mature religious thinkers had permitted crackpots to assume the role of pacifists in modern America and had thereby let pacifism fall into disrepute. It saddened him to see the pacifist caricatured as a pathetic idiot, or worse as a coward trying to save his self-respect by appealing to sentimental and confused ideals. Believing as he did that opposition to nuclear war was the modern Christian's most pressing task, and feeling that pacifism might well be the Christian's most effective weapon in his opposition, Merton was deeply disturbed by this false image of pacifism in the popular mind.[60]

Another traditional doctrine in need of reinterpretation, according to Merton, was the doctrine of just war, which he said could still be a positive and valuable guide to Christian ethical teachings on nuclear warfare even though many of its teachings were dated. Reinterpreted for the modern age the doctrine of just war could be an important aid in clarifying the Christian's ethical stance. Merton defined just war as "a *defensive* war in which force is strictly limited and the greatest care is taken to protect the rights and the lives of noncombatants and even of combatants.[61] These requirements had rarely been met by Christian armies, Merton argued, and they could hardly be met in a nuclear exchange of fire, for nuclear weapons are purely offensive, annihilating noncombatants and even neutrals, caring nothing for human life or health. Merton believed that if the conditions of just war were really made the guidelines for today's nuclear world, no nuclear war could begin. The old doctrine, reinterpreted in the light of modern circumstances, would perhaps help to save the world.

The doctrine of just war in Catholic theology is derived from the doctrine of natural law, and Merton appealed also to the natural law in calling for an end to nuclear buildup. Natural law, he explained, permits a man to defend himself and his family from aggression, to do violence even to the point of endangering the aggressor's life if this is clearly the last available resource. According to natural law, violence can be used in self-defense only at the moment of an assault that is intended to kill; if possible the aggressor must not be killed. Merton thus taught that while a nation may defend itself when attacked, it must not try to kill its opponent, which would happen if nuclear weapons were used.[62]

Still another doctrine of traditional Christian ethics which Merton wished to see reinterpreted and applied to the modern situation was the doctrine of Christian nonviolence. He warned that Christians must not just accept an inevitable nuclear holocaust; nor must they simply preach doom; nor must they begin to calculate how by a first-strike the "Christian West can eliminate communism for all time and usher in the millenium."[63] Instead, Christians must re-capture and reinterpret the doctrine of nonviolence, working actively but nonviolently for the total abolition of war. Merton admitted that nonviolence, just as pacifism, had been given a negative image and that Christians who practiced nonviolent protest against evil would be criticized by those who identified him as a Communist dupe or a "beatnik." He blamed Soviet propaganda, which had succeeded in convincing Americans that any call for disarmament was Communist treachery, for the typical American assumption that anyone who dared call for nuclear disarmament was either a Communist or a fellow traveler.[64] He also admitted that some of the nonviolent protest against nuclear war in this country had been shortsighted and immature, "more an expression of rebellion against the status quo in our own country than an effective opposition to war itself." He warned that the man who takes a naive and oversimplified position on nuclear war can easily be exploited by politicians of other nuclear powers and that the last thing a nuclear pacifist who is acting in nonviolent protest should do is start a war by aiding the effort of either side.[65] The true nonviolent nuclear pacifist, which Merton hoped would soon come to the fore in this country, would be a Christian who is well grounded in his own traditional theology and yet always open to discussion with men of other viewpoints.

Merton wanted a complete reinterpretation of the doctrine of prayer. He particularly disliked the slogan "Pray for Peace" which was being used to cancel stamps in this country in the 1950s and 1960s. Although he himself believed in praying for peace, he feared that this slogan would give many people a false sense of security, leading them to assume that a simple phrase on a letter could some-how protect them from nuclear attack. He also opposed stamping letters with a plea for prayer while at the same time spending billions of dollars on atomic submarines, thermonuclear weapons, and ballistic missiles, for he believed this to be hypocrisy and a mocking of God. He admitted the need for defense, saying that it is reasonable for a sick man to pray for good health and take medicine, but he felt that it was foolish for America to pray for peace and spend billions on weapons that would destroy the country, just as it would be foolish for someone to pray for good health and then drink poison.[66]

Merton himself often prayed for peace, praying that God would pacify not just the Russians and the Chinese but the Americans and himself as well. He prayed that both opponents in the cold war would be restored to sanity and would attack the world's problems together instead of preparing for global suicide.[67] He prayed for protection both from the Reds and from American folly and blindness, and while he admitted that praying for peace sounded archaic and sentimental, he found the scientific, political, and sociological answers of the day far less satisfactory.[68] He believed deeply in the power of prayer, but he felt that the entire doctrine needed to be reinterpreted and redefined if it were to be truly effective in the modern age.

He felt that the traditional Christian message, with all its attendant doctrines, was still valid and could provide a framework within which a Christian could approach the modern nuclear dilemma, but he longed to see this message reinterpreted and expressed in contemporary language. He also stressed the importance of acting out the message instead of just teaching it, saying that Christians should manifest the truths of the gospel in social actions and follow Jesus Christ in political commitments and social responsibilities as well as in penance and prayer. He called on Christians to act in society, not confining their political activities to the privacy and security of the polling booth, but helping to close the gap between interior intentions and external acts.[69]

Merton based his call to social action against nuclear war upon Pope John's first encyclical letter *Ad Petri Cathedram*. In this letter the pope called upon Christians to strive for peace without compromising with evil, without surrendering passively to injustice, and he identified the Christian vocation as the struggle in world affairs to establish Christ's peace. Merton responded by saying that since Christ is the Prince of Peace the church must indeed actively oppose the enemies of peace and salvation, according to the baptismal pledge.[70] The Christian, he said, must scrupulously avoid condoning or taking part in a nuclear war.[71] Pope John's letter also taught that the Christian must actively oppose evil, not try to achieve peace by passive acquiescence to evil, and Merton explained that Christ gives to his followers in every age the task of establishing peace in every heart and in every society. He called upon Christians to accept their task as peacemakers by helping men regain control over a world which, because of moral irresponsibility and military-scientific activism, was "speeding downhill without brakes." The Christian, in the tradition of Jesus, should bring the world not a tranquilizer but true peace, which must be won by active and positive opposition to evil.[72]

Merton's later writings contained numerous suggestions as to how Christians who understand their duty to preserve world peace might act out their faith in the world. He suggested that Christians help to create a general climate of rationality in the world, that they encourage the development of a humanistic outlook on life, one in which "rash and absurd assumptions" which lead to war would have little room to grow, an "atmosphere of sanity and trust in which negotiation and disarmament may eventually become feasible."[73] Because the use of nuclear power is essentially a moral problem, he said, the Christian must prepare the way for moral answers by creating an atmosphere in which an appropriate response of reason could be made. He suggested that Christians study the reports of scientists to understand the dangers of nuclear weapons, the speeches of political scientists to understand the meaning of world events, and the teachings of concerned religious leaders to determine how faith can be applied to these circumstances, and then help others to follow moral principles in their efforts toward peace.[74]

He also suggested that Christians avoid nationalism. He said that insofar as nationalism sets up the nation-state as the highest political object of man's allegiance, denying the principle of a higher order and divine justice, it is the "most retrograde movement the world has ever seen." He warned his readers that they must at all times be willing to admit that their political ideas are perhaps "illusions and fictions," pursued for reasons that are not completely honest. He distinguished, as did Pope Pius XII, between national life and nationalistic policies, the former being a combination of "the values which characterize a social group and enable it to contribute fruitfully to the whole polity of nations," while the latter are actions which pervert genuine national values by creating selfish and destructive strife between nations.[75] Believing that war would never be under control as long as nationalistic policies were in effect, Merton blamed nationalism for America's actions in Vietnam. Americans who see their country at the center of the universe, do business on their own terms, and impose their will upon all weaker nations, Merton said, have destroyed all opportunities for a lasting peace.[76]

Merton attempted to explode two related myths which he felt could lead America into war through sheer ignorance: the myth of the Christian West battling the atheistic East and the myth of the Good against the Bad. He explained that while there are untold thousands of Christians still living behind the iron curtain, most of the people in the West are no longer Christians in any meaningful sense of the word. And he reminded his readers that while the East does not profess Christian ethics they do have a type of humanism built into their political philosophy, while many times the West permits its materialistic and atheistic elements to replace its traditional Christian ethics. Neither side is all good or all evil, he said, and this very ambiguity should be enough to prevent a Christian from pursuing nationalistic policies or attitudes. He taught his readers to accept both East and West as a "mysterious, unaccountable mixture of good and evil,"[77] and he called for cooperation between East and West in trying to solve the dilemma of nuclear war, since no one had sufficient understanding or power to do so alone. He said: "I believe the basis for valid political action can only be the recognition that the true solution to our problems is *not* accessible to any one isolated party or nation but that all must arrive at it by working together."[78]

Merton said that while one's national citizenship and identity are important to his social and spiritual development, nationalism as an ideology can destroy the values which keep peace between men. He therefore proposed that a world state be planned and that men avoid rigid nationalism by building a "world federation of peaceful nations." He had little faith in the United Nations, but he felt that the only sane course open to the people of the world was "to work frankly and without compromise for a valid supernational authority and for the total abolition of war."[79] He envisioned an international authority with the power to control technology and convert its immense potential from making nuclear weapons to feeding and caring for men. Because he believed it to be a colossal farce to spend billions of dollars on weapons while two-thirds of the human race goes hungry, he said that Christians had no choice but to reject greedy and defensive nationalism and to work for the world state which could lay down its instruments of war and serve mankind. He elaborated: "a Christian who is not willing to envisage the creation of an effective international authority to control the destinies of man for peace is not acting and thinking as a mature member of the Church. He does not have fully Christian perspectives."[80]

Merton further advised Christians not to follow the leadership of any official whose actions were obviously unchristian. He explained that since modern warfare is planned and executed largely in secret by specialists, most people are at the mercy of their political leaders and that many have resigned themselves to a dangerous and blind faith in authority. He believed that Christians should constantly question the actions of their leaders to be sure they are acting morally and that they should be thoroughly acquainted with their nation's policies so as to judge whether they concur with Christian ethical teachings.[81] If a Christian is convinced that his leaders and their policies are wrong, illegal, or immoral, Merton said, he has the right and the duty to refuse them his allegiance. He taught that Christians must particularly resist the attempt of a state or its leaders to assume powers that God had not given them, particularly the power to destroy human life. He explained: "If the nation prepares to defend itself by methods that will almost certainly be immoral and illicit, then the Christian has *not only the right but also the duty* to question the validity of these methods, and to protest against them, even to the point of refusing his cooperation in their unjust and immoral use."[82] He realized that the refusal to follow the orders of established leaders might cost the Christian his position in society or even his life, but he reminded his readers that they were descended from the martyrs, who gave no forcible resistance but died willingly rather than worship the emperor. He advised them to imitate Jesus, who did not call twelve legions of angels but yielded to crucifixion, praying for his executioners. Merton said, in no uncertain terms, that the modern Christian is bound to "obey God rather than the state whenever the state tries to usurp powers that do not and cannot belong to it."[83]

In an essay entitled "A Devout Meditation in Memory of Adolf Eichmann" Merton pointed out that Christians cannot afford to follow their leaders blindly even when they are certain that their leaders are mentally sane. Psychiatrists had just declared that Eichmann, the Nazi leader who directed the extermination of six million Jews during World War II, was perfectly sane, and Merton explained that the sane men whose job it is to save mankind from barbarism and self-destruction are sometimes able to follow their sane logic to the legal explosion of a hydrogen bomb. He explained that sanity does not require love and that a leader can be perfectly sane and still consider love irrelevant, having no feelings for his fellowman. Love arises out of religion, is not necessarily natural, and has no necessary connection with sanity, but it is absolutely necessary for a man to be moral for a race to survive. "The one who cooly estimates how many millions of victims can be considered expendable in a nuclear war, I presume they do all right with the Rorschach ink blots too. On the other hand, you will probably find that the pacifists and the ban-the-bomb people are, quite seriously just as we read in *Time,* a little crazy."[84] Merton suggested that if world and national leaders were a little less "sane," a little more doubtful about right and wrong and more aware of the ethic of love, mankind might have a better chance to survive.[85]

Merton particularly warned Christians against following leaders who are militarily oriented. He felt that the main reason for the failure to make progress toward peace is that the world is led or intimidated by "military men, who are the blindest of the blind."[86] A subtle but devastating condemnation of military thinking in world affairs may be found in Merton's book *Original Child Bomb* which describes, in words "to be scratched on the walls of a cave" where the last survivors of a nuclear war are dying of radiation, the decision to drop the first atomic bomb on Hiroshima. He points out how the president's military advisers convinced him, with flawless military logic, that to drop an atomic bomb on two Japanese cities would bring a long-lasting peace to the world. The project was wrapped in theological terminology, with the test range named Trinity and the takeoff point called Papacy, but the logic of the operation was purely military. The Japanese generals, "professional soldiers" as Merton calls them, prevented their officials from asking for peace, and the American president's advisers, also professional soldiers, saw no moral evil in exploding the bomb. Merton feared that the same kind of people who started the nuclear arms race by bombing Hiroshima might one day end it with a logical attack on the enemy which would destroy the world.[87]

Merton, much to the dismay of many of his religious and secular readers, called upon Christians to refuse to work at any job that contributed to the making of nuclear weapons. He defended the

workers who took part in the peace strike of January 1962 and dedicated his mass on February 1, 1962, to such strikers everywhere in
the world, to all men who yearned for peace, and to those who
were working, praying, and sacrificing themselves for peace. He
expressed pity and a bit of contempt for the vast majority of Americans who could not understand the strike: "In their pitiful, blind
craving for undisturbed security, they feel that agitation for peace
is somehow threatening to them. They do not feel at all threatened
by the bomb, for some reason, but they feel terribly threatened by
some little girl student carrying a placard, or by some working man
striking in protest."[88]

He was convinced that the only way to start the journey toward
peace was to slow down the making of weapons of destruction. He
admitted that this was not the only solution and that alone it was
insufficient, but he said that it must be attempted even at the price
of economic and military sacrifices.[89] Presumably, if every Christian
should refuse to work in factories which contribute to the making
of nuclear weapons, this slowdown would occur. He aroused the
anger of many Catholics when he declared that the man who
works for a company which contributes to the nuclear buildup,
whether he makes bombs or not, is partially responsible for the
immorality of nuclear war. He angered many other Americans by
calling for a strike by all Christian and humanistic workers against
any company contributing directly or indirectly to the science of
nuclear war.[90] But he did not seem to mind the criticism, and he
continued to encourage workmen to decide against nuclear war
here and now, while there was still time, before they helped to
create any more potentially destructive instruments of war.[91]

In spite of his somewhat negative and hopeless analysis of the
world which he came to know in the 1950s and 1960s, Merton considered himself an optimist. His response to Pope John's encyclical
letter *Pacem in Terris* was perhaps his most explicit expression of
hope for man. He explained that the pope's letter was optimistic
and hopeful because he believed in the goodness of man. Pope
John, he said, dared believe that the goodness placed in man by
God the Creator is still in operation, and he therefore stood in direct opposition to the Machiavellian politicians who saw man as
depraved. Pope John could expect man to love and find peace,
while the Machiavellian could only expect man to deceive and use
force; Pope John could dare to hope for a new world based upon

man's innate goodness, while the Machiavellian's man could never build such a world.[92]

Merton stood proudly with Pope John on this issue, but he was not naively optimistic; he saw the ominous clouds on the horizon as clearly as any man of his day, and he understood that at any time one might mistakenly push the wrong button and destroy the world. He even described America's attitude as "utterly sinister, desperate, belligerent, illogical. We will either press the button or become fascists, in which case the button will be pressed all the more inevitably later on."[93] But in spite of his doubts, fears, and insight into the enormity of the problem, Merton dared to hope, advising his readers that they "must stand by the modicum of good that is in us without exaggerating it."[94] Merton believed that the majority of people on both sides wanted peace. He explained:

> Now that we have awakened to our fundamental barbarism, it seems to me that there is once again hope for a civilization, because men of good will want more than ever to be civilized. And now that we have our tremendous capacities for evil staring us in the face, there is more incentive than ever for men to become saints. For man is naturally inclined to good, and not to evil. Besides our nature, we have what is infinitely greater—the grace of God, which draws us powerfully upward to the infinite Truth and is refused to no one who desires it.[95]

Merton based his hope for man, a hope which seems a bit foreign to his previous pessimism, upon the doctrine of the Incarnation, the teaching that God became man in order to save men.[96] Whether he was attempting to regain the orthodoxy of his early days, turned to this doctrine for consolation in his despair, or truly believed in the goodness of man, the optimism at the heart of Catholic theology eventually won out in Merton's thought. He charged Christians: "Be human in this most inhuman of ages; guard the image of man for it is the image of God."[97] He called on Christians to believe in God and man, name nuclear war the evil that it is, and work toward world union.

Chapter Five

The Grim Reaper
of Violence

When Thomas Merton emerged from his monastic hideaway in the early 1950s and looked again upon the America which he had adopted, he saw a land filled with violence, a society whose personality and nature were molded by its violent past and whose inability to change its violent present might cause it to be destroyed. The violence to which he referred more and more often in his later writings was not simply crime in the streets but something which he believed afflicted the whole structure of American life which, while outwardly ordered and respectable, was inwardly chaotic. It was the violence which had chased him into the cloister, a violence which had increased rather than decreased during his exile.

The racial crisis and the war in Vietnam were for Merton simply the visible signs of America's more basic violence: "white collar violence, the systematically organized bureaucratic and technological destruction of man."[1] He constantly expressed the fear that America's great accomplishments might be neutralized and her idealistic personality perverted by this disease of violence. In a paper written at the request of the National Commission on the Causes and Prevention of Violence Merton said that the real source of American violence is in American culture itself, its mass media, its competitiveness, and its inflated myths of virility, in its preoccupation with nuclear, chemical, bacteriological, and psychological overkill.[2]

Merton believed that the most obvious and continuing sign of America's violence was the racism which had led to her greatest social crisis of the 1960s. Believing that the same violent dynamic separated black and white in this country and East and West in world affairs, he warned that America's racial attitudes were as potentially destructive as her cold war attitudes. He feared a racial war between Americans of different races almost as much as he feared a nuclear war between ideological opponents.

His interest in racial matters was not a concern characteristic of only the latter part of his career. As a graduate student in the early 1940s he visited Harlem and for a time considered working in Baroness de Hueck's mission, and before entering the monastery he was already writing of the dangers of America's segregated society. One example of his early concern is the following poem of social protest. It describes in vivid terminology Merton's understanding of the conditions which would lead to racial revolution twenty years later:

> Across the cages of the keyless aviaries,
> The lines and wires, the gallows of the broken kites,
> Crucify, against the fearful light,
> The ragged dresses of the little children.
> Soon, in the sterile jungles of the waterpipes and ladders,
> The bleeding sun, a bird of prey, will terrify the poor,
> Who will forget the unbelievable moon.
>
> But in the cells and wards of white buildings,
> Where the glass dawn is brighter than the knives of surgeons,
> Paler than alcohol or ether,
> Greyer than guns and shinier than money,
> The white men's wives, like Pilate's,
> Cry in the peril of their frozen dreams:
>
> "Daylight has driven iron spikes,
> Into the flesh of Jesus' hands and feet:
> Four flowers of blood have nailed Him to the walls of Harlem."[3]

Throughout his career, from the early responses to Harlem through the discussions of Gandhi and Martin Luther King to his late poetry of universal scope, Merton consistently and insistently blamed the racial crisis in America on the white man. In a review of *The Shoshoneans,* a book concerning the white man's treatment of the Shoshonean Indians, he explained in prose what he later expressed so superbly in the poetic *Geography of Lograire:*

that white men in every corner of the globe have sought to make slaves of darker peoples and have for the most part succeeded. After enslaving them physically, he went on, they enslave them emotionally by forcing upon them a servitude and helplessness which makes them forever inferior to their conquering landlords. The white man forces other peoples to accept an invented identity, and he must not be surprised when he is repaid in kind.[4] Crime in the ghetto, which is called violence, is simply the result of the violence of injustice which creates ghettos in the first place.[5]

Merton believed that the American white man, who has afflicted the American Negro with his prejudice, is perhaps even more unjust and violent than white men in other parts of the world because of his fear of imminent social disruption. The British colonial could grant his slaves their freedom and return home, leaving the land if not the money in their hands, but the white American shares his own soil with his slaves.

Moreover, he explained, just when white America was least able, because of the pressures of the cold war, to cope with the Negro's march toward full equality, the Negro decided to make himself conspicuous. The result was on the one hand a pathetic but audible rush of liberal concern in response to the Negro's call for help and on the other the emergence of a tightened resistance from those who "blame someone else for their own inner inadequacies." Merton predicted that this inability or refusal to listen to the Negro's demands, coupled with an incredibly inhuman determination to keep him down at all costs, would inevitably create a "hopelessly chaotic and violent revolutionary situation" in America's future. He concluded that if the Negro were to rebel and precipitate a destructive revolution, future historians would blame white America for its refusal to acknowledge its injustice.[6]

Merton, in the tradition of Frederick Douglas, saw the Negro problem as a white problem, the result of the white man's refusal to listen to the Negro. If the white man had truly listened to the Negro's call for justice, he surmised, he would have joined the revolution, rejecting his former prejudice, but he was afraid to listen, knowing intuitively that his prosperity was rooted in injustice and that to listen would be to renounce his ill-gotten gain.[7]

Merton was of course severely criticized for blaming the white man for all the racial strife in this country, and in an article written just before his death he admitted that while few white men personally mistreat Negroes, almost every white man lives under a system that is unjust to the Negro and thus contributes to a social order that relegates him to an inferior station in life. The very white man who thinks he is being fair to the Negro treats him as an inferior human being who will receive the fruits of white generosity so long as he keeps in his place, the place of an inferior. Therefore, Merton concluded that it is "necessary for a man who wants to be in good faith to cease identifying himself with actions that are causing the evil in question, and to disclaim any intention of further participating in these acts, while also doing whatever he can to restore the balance of justice and of violated rights."[8] But the contemporary racial crisis, Merton believed, grew also out of the white man's unconscious desire to be punished for his past injustice. Angered by nonviolent marches toward freedom because they create the image of a wronged and nonaggressive Negro, the white man in Merton's descriptions tries to provoke the Negro into using violent methods to achieve his ambitions so that his own self-image will not be further injured.[9]

Merton was certain that white America's violence against its Negro population had hurt its prestige abroad. He called on America to prove its faith in such doctrines as the worth of the individual and equal rights under law by granting them to the Negro.

He believed that America's violence and hypocrisy in the field of human rights had clearly influenced its recent military policies, which were based upon the call for peace and freedom for the whole world but which allowed for the possible destruction of all mankind in the very name of peace and freedom. The world had lost faith in America, Merton argued, because Americans defend the principle of human rights rather than human beings, a policy long evident in its racial affairs. America had for so long claimed to respect the Negro as a person while lynching him or pressing him into the ghetto without seeing the contradiction that it naturally tended to follow the same pattern in world affairs, where other nations could see the hypocrisy and name it for what it was. In theory America defended the Negro's rights just as in theory it defended the rights of all peoples to peace and freedom, Merton said, but in practice it had abandoned both theory and practice. This basic contradiction, Merton concluded, would eventually destroy America's already deteriorating reputation as a moral leader of nations. Merton theorized that other nations were growing more and more hostile toward America because they were beginning to realize that white Americans are more interested in profits than in persons. White America's response to the Negro revolution had proved that in America business was freer than men, for only when Negro protests touched the white man's pocket book were they taken seriously.[10]

From the very beginning of his involvement in the racial crisis of the 1960s, Merton was pessimistic about the future of racial harmony in America. Blaming the trouble on the white American's arrogance, fear, injustice, and hypocrisy, he believed the picture would grow increasingly darker. In a "Letter to a White Priest" in the early 1960s he warned against the assumption that racial problems could be solved easily or quickly, and he rejected the optimistic hope that the Negro would take his equal place in American society with just a little more time, legislation, editorializing, and goodwill. He even predicted that many white people would be driven back in fear to blind, violent reaction and that increased white injustice would lead to ever more Negro violence, which in turn would give rise to an American brand of Nazism.[11]

Because he felt that the church must be concerned with all human crises, he began to call on Catholics to take a bold stand on racial justice. This was in the late 1950s, just as soon as he had surveyed and determined the seriousness of the situation. He was certain that the church was losing influence within the Negro community because of its failure to take a stand, and he labeled as naive and evasive the church's pattern of making an occasional pious moral statement while cautioning the Negro to go slow. He believed that the loss of Christian influence in the civil rights movement, which he seemed to perceive much earlier than most churchmen, was due to white Christians' inadequate and sometimes even false conception of the racial problem. He said that most white Christians believed that the Negro's only ambition was to be a white man and that the church should advance the Negroes generously. Even worse, according to Merton, many Catholics saw the South as a vast pool of potential Negro converts and were sending a white apostolate to turn them into imitation white Catholics, an act which repelled the Negro, especially when he learned that he could not worship in every Catholic church in the South and that in some he could receive communion only after white Catholics had left the sanctuary. Merton called these naive attitudes and practices parodies of true Catholicism, and he scorned their assumption of white superiority and desire to integrate Negroes into white Christianity by imposing white ways upon them. The truly Christian approach, he argued, would be to assume the complete equality of the two races and acknowledge that their cultures are correlative, that they mutually complement each other: "The white man is for the black man: that is why he is white. The black man is for the white man: that is why he is black."[12]

Although Merton warned against naive optimism about America's racial crisis long before the disillusionment of the mid-1960s and for a time received criticism from those who foresaw a peaceful integration of the races, he himself mirrored this optimism by cautiously writing about one ray of hope that he saw in the gloom. He too lauded the congressional victories and successful marches, and he dared to hope that the Negro and the white man would eventually realize their mutual need for each other and become brothers. His hope lay in the vibrations he felt in the writings of new Negro novelists, among them James Baldwin. Baldwin, whom Merton described as a genuinely religious writer, was then teaching through his novels that no man is racially or socially complete within himself, that no man has in himself *"all* the excellence of all humanity." Baldwin's well-expressed belief that no man is completely human until he has found his European, African, or Asian brother led Merton to hope that Baldwin's message would be understood and accepted by all Americans; if so, there was reason to hope for racial peace and understanding.[13] He began to encourage his white readers to support the Negro's movement toward dignity and liberty without trying to run the movement, and he advised them to support such nonviolent Christian leaders as Martin Luther King, Jr., accepting with love the changes which the revolution would bring to American life. He cautiously dared to hope that white America would listen in time.[14]

He also read with interest the novel *A Different Drummer* by William Melvin Kelly, who perhaps unconsciously expressed the biblical concept of *kairos,* the appointed time. Merton found this concept, which originally referred to the time of salvation in the advent of Christ, fitting for the present moment in the civil rights movement; it was an announcement that the time of liberation had come and that it was a time of salvation for black and white alike. In Kelly's book Tucker Caliban, a southern Negro sharecropper, burned his house and quietly left the state. One by one other Negro families followed him, leaving finally only one Negro, a northern Black Supremist, who was then lynched by the frustrated whites. This literary departure and complete disappearance of the Negroes was for Merton a symbolic statement of their final rejection of paternalism, tutelage, and servitude. It was the announcement that the Negro's hour of destiny had arrived, and it was a final, healthy, definitive rejection of white America's social order.[15] It left Merton with a sense of hope, for it made him believe that the Negro's rejection of further injustice had made possible this *kairos* in which whites and Negroes would have "a unique and momentous opportunity to repair this injustice and to reestablish the violated moral and social order on a new plane."

In those days, the mid-1960s, Merton taught that the *kairos* would be an hour of salvation and freedom for both the white man and the Negro. The white man who would listen to the Negro's message would be released from the bondage of prejudice and fear just as the Negro would be released from the bondage of economic and psychological slavery. Merton was cautiously optimistic when he read the speeches of nonviolent Christian spokesmen like Dr. King, for they expressed love for the white man as well as for the black. Basing their ideals upon the teachings of Mahatma Gandhi and Jesus Christ, these men were striving for truth even before their own liberty, and they sought to save the white man's soul by showing him his injustice toward the Negro at the same time that they were liberating their own people. They could have, like Tucker Caliban, walked away and left the white man in his hell of violence and hate, but they had accepted the mission of using the *kairos* to save America's soul, its white side as well as its black. They were willing to suffer like Christ for "the liberation of the Negro and the redemption of the white man, blinded by his endemic sin of racial injustice."[16]

Inspired by such self-sacrifice, Merton reminded Americans that they lived not in the world of Aeschylus and Sophocles, where the aspiration to freedom brought guilt and punishment from the gods, but in the world of Jesus Christ where man is liberated and redeemed by an inner truth that makes him obey the Lord of History.[17] Following the ideal of Jesus Christ, he said, the Negro leaders of the early 1960s were acting to heal a society rent by racism and to achieve unity in reconciliation. They were seeking by sacrifice and love to redeem the white man, to enlighten him so that he would save his own soul by initiating the reforms which alone could save American society.[18] After comparing the "spiritual earnestness" of the Negro leaders and novelists with the "fumbling evasions and inanities" of their opponents and critics, Merton accepted their message as the word of truth for modern man, saying with them that the *kairos,* the moment of freedom, had come. The time of salvation and liberation came and went for black, white, and Thomas Merton in 1964.[19]

But even in those early, optimistic days, before he discovered that fiction is never as brutal as fact and that social mores are more powerful than Christian ideals, Merton warned that the white man might refuse to respond positively to the Negro's announcement of the *kairos.* Indeed, he predicted as early as 1963 that if the *kairos* passed unheeded, it would be followed by an hour of destruction and hatred. The Negro "will no longer be the gentle, wide-eyed child singing hymns while dogs lunge at his throat. There will be no more hymns and no more prayer vigils. He will become a Samson whose African strength flows ominously back into his arms. He will suddenly pull the pillars of white society crashing down upon himself and his oppressor."[20]

He used the following legend from the life of Mohammed to illustrate the importance of the white man's response to the black announcement of the *kairos.* Mohammed, who was seeking a religious faith, visited a colony of Nestorian Christians in Arabia to ask them for a sign of the truth of their faith. To test them he asked them to walk on red-hot coals, but they refused and called him mad for suggesting such a thing. He left them and later, in the burning desert heat, came to "a truth of stark and dreadful simplicity—to be proved by the sword."[21] Merton believed that the Negro, represented by the outsider Mohammed, was asking white society, the Nestorians, for a sign of good faith which would permit him to believe in America. If the white man would not respond to the challenge, which might well require painful sacrifices, the Negro would turn to a different philosophy, one which might well raise the sword of violence to destroy the existing order. Merton's prediction, which at the time was scorned by optimists, has proved correct in more recent days.

As he observed the increasing militance of younger Negroes and the stubborn resistance of white men to the call for freedom,

Merton grew ever more pessimistic about the future of the civil rights movement, and his writings reflected his changing mood. Just after the passage of the Civil Rights Bill of 1964 he commented that the bill, while good, was a mere piece of paper in places where the social majority opposed it. He believed that in spite of the bill, or perhaps because of it, the civil rights movement would enter a new and more critical phase in which the Negro, to exercise his new legal rights, would grasp for "some kind of power." The white men who had worked long and hard in the movement would then become disenchanted with the new militant spirit and would join his white conservative brothers to form a united front of resistance to the movement.[22]

It was at this time that he began to plead for white men to step aside and place all their hope for really constructive and positive results in the freed hands of the Christian nonviolent Negro leaders. He feared that white control of the movement had already injured the prestige of its Negro leaders, and he predicted that they would soon lose control: "as the movement gains in power, the reasonableness and the Christian or at least ethical fervor of the elements will recede into the background and the movement will become more and more an unreasoning and intransigeant mass movement dedicated to the conquest of sheer power, more and more inclined to violence."[23] A tougher Negro leadership would probably emerge, he predicted, one that would not believe in moderation or nonviolence, one that would effectively use the threat of force embodied in the great concentration of angry, unemployed Negroes in northern city ghettos. The truth of Merton's prediction is only now becoming fully evident.

After 1964 Merton's comments on the civil rights movement became consistently more pessimistic. He began to say that Americans might well have missed the *kairos,* that the moment of truth was certainly gone, and that the American scene would become more and more one of "darkness, anarchy, and moral collapse."[24] Yet he still hoped for America's salvation. His last major statement on the racial crisis, an article called "The Hot Summer of Sixty-Seven," called upon whites and Negroes to unite to work for total equality, regardless of the price, for this was the only hope for peace between the races. He admitted the hopelessness of this request unless a deep renewal of Christian conscience occurred among both whites and blacks, but he still dared hope for such a renewal. His earlier prediction, that time was running out for the success of a peaceful revolution, had been proved correct as the Black Power movement replaced the Christian nonviolent movement. He then predicted that unless the renewal of conscience came soon violence would take over and the black movement would become "more and more aimless, nihilistic, arbitrary, destructive and non-amenable to reasonable control."[25]

Just as Merton blamed the racial crisis in America on the white man who insisted on enslaving the Negro and keeping him a child and servant, so he blamed the worsening of the crisis upon the white liberal who even more than the white conservative should be held responsible for the darkening civil rights picture. Although he was himself a white man and a liberal, he had little respect for the "white liberal," a breed of white men who, in Merton's terminology, differ from the white conservative or the white Christian. Merton had little faith in the white liberal's racial attitudes and practices because the white liberal assumed that he understood the Negro when he actually did not and could not. The Negro, he said, knows a reality which no white man will ever know, "things which belong to the pure, unique, spiritual destiny of America," things which only the Negro and the Indian can know because of their suffering. White liberals, naively believing that they understood the Negro, confused the racial situation by giving the impression that Negroes really had a nice place waiting for them in white society, and Merton pointed out that just the opposite was true. For example, he said, the presence of white people in the march on Washington in 1963 probably hurt the Negro cause by creating the illusion that white society was open to blacks when in reality the black man is an outcast from American society. The optimism produced by this false illusion simply strengthened the inertia of those who lived comfortably in the status quo, a social structure in which the Negro had no place at all. Since the purpose of the march was to demonstrate the ostracism of the Negro from American society, white liberals actually distorted its whole meaning.[26]

Merton always portrayed the white liberal as ignorant of his own motives, ignorant of the Negro's feelings, and ignorant of the meaning of the civil rights movement. The white liberal, he said, did not understand when he was "helping" the Negro in 1963 that if the Negro should enter fully into American life the entire society would be radically altered; property values, the tone and tempo of life, business and the professions, labor relations, and popular psychology would all be changed. The white conservative knew this and fought it, but the white liberal did not even understand it.[27] He assumed that the Negro would "fit in" to white middle class-dom, not realizing that the Negro would destroy all current political and social patterns by changing the life-style and electing other Negroes to high offices.[28] Merton scorned the liberal who wanted the Negro to have rights so long as they did not threaten his own, and he had little respect for the liberal northern legislators who with great zeal made laws about integration in the South while permitting discrimination in their own cities.[29]

Merton pointed out that while the white liberal was encouraging the Negro, the Negro knew that his white friend did not really care for him as a person, that the white liberal was following the traditional pattern of defending a cause rather than a human being. The white liberal, so comfortable in the Establishment, was using him for a cause, and he knew it. He knew that the liberal wanted a place in the civil rights movement so that he could apply the brakes when his interests were threatened and that when his demands got too stringent his friend would sell him down the river. Merton predicted that the white liberal of 1962 would suddenly awaken to realize that the future of the civil rights movement was entirely out of his control, that he was not prepared for such a dreadful future, and that the movement must be slowed. He would change his political philosophy to conservative and begin buying rifles for his white brothers. Seeing his world being cut away, he would probably charge that the Communists are behind all the racial trouble and begin to encourage forceful suppression of the Negro. Merton's concluding portrait of the white liberal's future actions is mercilessly painted: "I visualize you, my liberal friend, goosestepping down Massachusetts Avenue in the uniform of an American Totalitarian Party in a mass rally where nothing but the most uproarious approval is manifest, except, by implication, on the part of silent and strangely scented clouds of smoke drifting over from the new 'camps' where the 'Negroes are living in retirement.' "[30]

Martin Marty, a Protestant theologian who reviewed the book *Seeds of Destruction* in which this statement appeared, spoke for many of Merton's readers when he accused him of overstating the dangers of the white liberal and the civil rights movement in general. He thought Merton's pessimism unjustified and felt that an isolated monk should not intimidate the positive activities of well-intentioned men, even if they were acting out of subconscious and perhaps not always Christian motivations. Later however, in an open letter to Merton published in the *National Catholic Reporter,* Marty apologized for the bad review and admitted that Merton's predictions were coming true. He agreed that things would get worse before they got better, that the Negro had indeed lost faith in the white man, and that the white liberal was confused and in danger of turning against the revolting Negro. He applauded Merton's wisdom and perception and asked him to suggest a constructive role for white liberals to play in this new civil rights movement. Merton answered Marty, also in an open letter, by saying that the white liberal, if sincerely concerned, could begin to work behind the scenes for the Negro, desiring no recognition or thanks. The white liberal of the future, in order to prove his sincerity, would be required to give a Christian nonviolent response to violence.[31] And because, as he indicates in *The Geography of Lograire,* whiteness is more an attitude than a color, the white liberal can do something about the disaster which his own kind have created. "Certainly America seems to have lost much in World War II. It has come out a bloated, suspicious, truculent militarist and one who is not without paranoid tendencies: yet there are in America also, fully alive and fully creative, some of the best tendencies of European independence and liberal thought. No matter how we may criticize Europe and America, they are still in full strength, and in their liberal minority the hope of the future still lies."[32]

But Merton clearly feared a white reaction to the more militant black of the late 1960s, a reaction to Negro violence which would lead to a Nazi-type American government. A successful Negro revolution would be impossible unless America were crippled by a major disaster, he explained, and militant Negroes might succeed only in creating such panic and disorder that a police state would be established. He feared that white extremists from former liberal as well as conservative camps might take over such a government, ruling by irrational and arbitrarily violent means, even building extermination camps for Negroes and then for any other "undesirable" elements within the society. In a review of Bernd Naumann's *Auschwitz* Merton declared that there were many people who would respond to an American Hitler. As normal people, not giants or insane, just like the managers of Auschwitz, they would keep the crematories running smoothly and efficiently. Recalling the smiling faces of the Mississippians who murdered three young civil rights workers, he warned that given the right kind of racial crisis, Nazis could blossom out all over the country.[33]

Merton had for many years called upon the church to declare itself for the Negro's march toward equality, and when the crisis deepened his call became louder and more emphatic. He said that while the Negro had lost faith in Christianity the Christian must not turn his back upon the Negro in disgust or timid pessimism. The white Christian must act as the white liberal was incapable of acting. In what might be thought of as his last statement to racist America, Merton preached: "There is no white and black in Christ: but if Christianity is being discredited in the eyes of Negroes, that does not dispense us from our duty to be authentic Christians toward the Negro whether he likes us or not."[34] The Christian, he said, should neither manufacture Molotov cocktails nor try to convert black power to nonviolence but should find, identify, and help eliminate injustice, which is the root of Negro violence. He concluded: "Black Power or no Black Power, I for one remain *for* the Negro. I trust him, I recognize the overwhelming justice of his complaint, I confess I have no right whatever to get in his way, and that as a Christian I owe him support, not in his ranks but in my own among the whites who refuse to trust him or hear him, and who want to destroy him."[35]

Thus Merton left his last will and testament to an America whose racial crisis of the 1960s foreshadowed an even greater crisis in the 1970s. He was prescient about the causes, nature, and development of the civil rights upheaval all through the 1960s: in his early warnings of the seriousness of the Negro's march toward liberty and the possibility of a white Nazi-type reaction; in his cautious optimism in 1964, when legislative victories opened one avenue of escape from disaster; in his approval of the nonviolent protest marches and demonstrations and of the Negro novelists' themes; in his pessimism, or perhaps it should be called realism, of the late 1960s when he realized that the white man had destroyed his chances of solving the problem of racial justice. He was right in his evaluation of the white man, and especially the white liberal without Christian or at least humanitarian convictions, and the Negro. He gained the attention and respect of such diverse black leaders as Martin Luther King, Jr., whose plan to visit Merton at Gethsemani was dissolved by his death in Memphis, and Eldridge Cleaver, who discussed Merton in his famous *Soul on Ice*. He stood on the cutting edge of history, understanding and correctly interpreting recent developments and looking into the future to prophesy about coming events. He left a grand example for the white Christian to follow in the 1970s.

Merton believed that the violence which had manifested itself so clearly in America's racial crisis was also evident in its most pressing international problem of the 1960s: the war in Vietnam. He once said, "It is perfectly logical that the America of L.B.J. should be at once the America of the Vietnam war and the Detroit riots. It's the same America, the same violence, the same slice of mother's cherry pie."[36] This violence, which seemed to break forth at every possible moment, was ravaging Merton's America from within and from without during his last years, and he attempted to expose it so that it could be eradicated. He opposed both racial injustice and the war with equal zeal, hoping that he and like-minded men could enlighten America before she destroyed herself. His statements were often little more than fingers in the dike, but behind them always lay positive suggestions for the dike's complete reconstruction.

Merton was one of the first thinkers and writers to see the relationship between the escalation of the war in Vietnam and the racial disturbances in America. He believed that the Negro, seeing each night on television the white American Establishment's suppression of both the Negro in the ghetto and the Vietnamese peasant in his hamlet, had begun to change his entire attitude toward white America. The American Negro, he explained, came to see the war as a contest between Asian colored people and white colonials who were invading their land, the Viet Cong being colored freedom fighters bravely battling the giant white technological power. As a result many Negroes were leaving the struggle for civil rights, concluding that the Christian nonviolence of King was futile idealism, and declaring guerrilla warfare on white America. Since the white man seemed to understand nothing but violence, Merton said, the young black militants had determined to burn and terrorize him just as he had burned and terrorized the Vietnamese.[37]

Merton argued that the war in Vietnam, like all wars in which America would likely be engaged during this dangerous period in man's history, was caused not by a threat to America itself or even to its ideals but by a threat to its wealth and power. America wrongly assumed that its wealth and prestige were being threatened in Vietnam, he said, and it covered up its selfishness by maintaining that its ideals were being threatened and that its government in Saigon was the guardian of liberty. He said that so few American leaders have opposed the war because, being personally involved in it, they could not bear to admit that young lives had been sacrificed in order to "bolster up the power of politicians and the wealth of the big corporations." It was not easy, he pointed out, for American leaders to admit that its sons, fathers, and brothers had died in vain, and so the pretense had continued, rendering Americans impotent to call the war a fraud and criminal.[38] The violence of selfishness and falsehood had already cost almost 30,000 young American lives by the time of Merton's own death, and he literally cried out for its end.

In his last major book on social affairs, *Faith and Violence,* Merton devoted an entire section to the war in Vietnam, calling it "an overwhelming atrocity." He described the death of innocent men, women, and children, sometimes from the horrible napalm, and concluded that the war was actually strengthening communism's appeal in southeast Asia by making the Viet Cong appear to be a gallant force of natives fighting against the hated and violent enemy, the opponents of the people. Merton, always a pacifist, declared that the war in Vietnam was the worst mistake in man's military history, calling it an extension of America's frontier mentality of always wanting to subdue an "inferior" race, but he used it as just another example of mankind's addiction to war. Just as an alcoholic who knows that drink will kill him continues to drink and even to find good reasons for doing so, he explained, so does mankind continue to fight and even justify the fighting which could eventually kill everyone.[39] The war in Vietnam was for Merton an indication of the worsening of a moral cirrhosis of the liver.

One obvious characteristic of Merton's social criticism, both of the world and of American society, was his tendency to oversimplify. He presented only the facts about the cold war and the racial crisis that supported his own theories and seemed not even to understand some of the complex issues involved in these problems, blaming the cold war simply on Americanism and racial strife only on the white man's sin. And he tended to blame those who were most like himself for world and national problems, enjoying a contempt for his own identity groups. An American himself, he blamed Americans for the cold war; a white liberal himself, he blamed the white man, and especially the liberal, for racial conflict and injustice. He was certainly lacking in a trained historical sense, seeming not to understand the different historical developments of America and Germany which would mitigate against a Nazi government's being established in this country. Merton's culprits tended to be his own kind, who alone were responsible for most of mankind's problems, who would eventually probably destroy the good achievements of man, whether that seemed historically likely or not.

But in spite of, or perhaps because of, his oversimplification Merton succeeded in pointing up some real faults in American life, faults which have certainly contributed to the problems of the world and society. He may have purposely oversimplified his statements at times for their effect, since he once expressed admiration for Dominican theology which, though he admitted oversimplified complex issues, did paint clearly the message of Christ to a rather blind world. His sometimes simplistic criticisms of Americans and white liberals are perhaps examples of this purposive oversimplification. Neither of these groups is as insensitive, unreasonable, or dangerous as Merton thought, but they do have faults and should be able to profit by Merton's criticism. The prophets, from Amos and Teiresias to Reinhold Niebuhr and Thomas Merton, have always most clearly seen and most adequately described the sins of their own kind.

Merton's genius lay in his ability to look beyond the facts of everyday life to the larger meanings of events and in his ability to express these meanings in language that lived on in the minds of his readers. His skills, put to a severe test by the confusion of the modern world, served him well during the 1960s as he tried to understand what was wrong with American society and what might be done to remedy the problems caused by American violence. He was one of the few who seemed to be on top of events and to provide answers which, while not always popular, were in almost every case substantially correct. His language was of course both a blessing and a curse. It grasped his readers' attention and drew them into discussions of ultimate questions. His gift of words and talent in expressing controversial ideas made him a gadfly who stirred up healthy conversation and genuine dialogue. On the other hand, his words certainly inflamed the passions of his readers. A man of lesser talent might have made the same basic points that Merton made in a more detached and moderate way. There was no moderate response to Merton, whether he was writing on contemplation or social issues, and his readers usually accepted his theories without question or rejected them out of hand. More moderate language might well have made fewer enemies and more thoughtful admirers.

But regardless of the language used, the accuracy of what he wrote is unquestioned. His predictions about America's racial crisis, his advice to the church about what position to take on the moral issues of the day, and his analysis of the cause and future course of the war in Vietnam have all proved incisive and prophetic. His solution to the violence which is seen on every hand, while not new or unique to him, was just as correct and prophetic as his other ideas and is worthy of serious contemplation. He espoused the doctrine of Christian nonviolent resistance against injustice and violence, advocating and explaining to Catholics and secularists the philosophy of Mahatma Gandhi and Martin Luther King, Jr. Admitting that other measures would also be necessary, he stated that if enough wise and well-intentioned men would dedicate themselves to this doctrine, violence at home and abroad would cease.

Merton believed that the Vietnam conflict, racial strife, and the cold war had the same basic composition; the ideological struggle between East and West which had led to the threshold of nuclear war was to him similar in nature to the American racial crisis which had led to the threshold of social disruption because they both indicated that the fabric of world and national life was torn to such an extent that if the tear were not repaired annihilation was imminent. Merton's concern as a Christian monk living in the

1960s was to repair these torn fabrics and heal the wounds of a violent and separative past. The only philosophy and method which he believed capable of restoring unity to American and world affairs, of mending the fabric and healing the wounds caused by racism and militarism, was the Christian philosophy of non-violent protest against injustice and war. Merton's own decision to enter a monastery in the early 1940s was a nonviolent protest against the chaos and disunity of man's society, and the mature monk of the 1960s felt justified in recommending it to men of good will in every circumstance of life.

Merton constantly protested modern man's tendency to accept passively the violence of his day without attempting to overcome it, and he called upon his readers to admit their violence without acquiescing to it. He was incensed by the thesis of Robert Ardrey's *African Genesis,* which he reviewed just after its publication in this country. Criticizing Ardrey's slavish commitment to an ironbound determinism which sees man as descended from the killer ape and therefore in his most natural pose with a club in his hand, Merton concluded, "It is one thing to admit our violence and face it humbly and realistically: quite another to turn that 'acceptance' into the shouting and posturing of racist self-congratulations."[40] He suggested that the book might win some favor in America, with all its rampant glorification of violence, but not in Europe where such glorification of man's violent nature had already led to two destructive wars in this century.

For Merton, the antidote to this praise of human folly was a human, nonviolent response. But he knew that nonviolence would have a hard time gaining support because of the "largely negative and completely inadequate" understanding of the philosophy of nonviolence shared by most Americans. While he believed that nonviolence is based upon the concepts of meekness and humility which Jesus preached in the Sermon on the Mount, he admitted that most Americans think of it as unchristian, ineffectively weak, or characteristic of the mentally ill, or perhaps all three of these at once. To prove his point, he quoted a weekly newsmagazine's description of Lee Harvey Oswald, the accused assassin of President Kennedy, as "inclined to non-violence up to a point where his mind snapped." Oswald, Merton countered, did not believe in non-violence at all, but the public accepted apparently without question the assumption that his diseased mind could just as easily espouse nonviolence as assassination. Merton was disturbed that so many Americans had embraced a myth which regarded nonviolence, the one modern philosophy which he believed appealed directly to the Gospels, as basically unchristian while regarding force and violence as normal and proper.[41]

Because Merton was so thoroughly convinced of the validity of nonviolent protest as a remedy for modern man's woes, and because of such mass misunderstanding of the philosophy, he spent a great deal of time during the last five years of his life trying to make clear to Americans that nonviolence, rather than attacking the ideals of Christianity and democratic society, actually fulfilled and implemented these ideals. He called upon Americans to free themselves of their mythical and inadequate self-understanding, largely derived from television westerns in which white Americans were portrayed as gun-toting frontiersmen, and return to their professed ideals of peace, love, and justice. His pleas reached the level of eloquence and helped to create a practical, descriptive philosophy upon which a modern Christian could build his program of social action.

Merton argued that those who have accepted nonviolence as a philosophy and method, steeping themselves in its principles and programs and then acting out those principles in their lives, had proved by their great deeds the truth and validity of the nonviolent approach to social problems. He admired such witnesses as the Jesuit Alfred Delp, who refused to lend priestly support to the Nazis; Franz Jagerstatter, who refused to fight with the Nazi army, even after his bishop pleaded with him to join up; and Simone Weil, whose ideas intrigued and challenged Merton's own mind and helped convert him to nonviolence. These people and many others like them, he said, had proved that nonviolent protest is not only one way of attacking injustice but is the most successful and possibly the only really effective way to fight social injustice and evil. Even the distortions of the news media which he personally distrusted, he said, could not detract from their witness.[42]

In the field of racial affairs Merton singled out the work of Martin Luther King, Jr., as the most Christian and effective plan for achieving racial and national unity. In the field of international affairs he most admired the work of King's guiding spirit, Mahatma Gandhi. Merton's admiration for Gandhi, who initiated the modern nonviolent protest movement through his resistance to

British rule in India, was revealed in a number of articles and one major book which he edited toward the end of his life.

Merton gained his understanding of nonviolence from Gandhi's writings, and he taught his readers nonviolence by interpreting Gandhi's teachings to them. He called Gandhi the first of the few modern men who have personally fulfilled the most urgent task of the twentieth century: the synthesis of East and West, which was Merton's own dream. Merton believed that since neither the ancient wisdoms of the Orient nor the modern sciences of the Occident are complete and satisfying to man without the other and since modern communications have made the union of East and West possible, the primary task of modern man was to bring these two worlds together: "Wisdom without science is unable to penetrate the full sapiential meaning of the created and material cosmos. Science without wisdom leaves man enslaved to a world of unrelated objects in which there is no way of discovering (or creating) order and deep significance in man's own pointless existence."[43]

Gandhi, Merton believed, was the first and greatest modern man. By living in both worlds and understanding both societies, East and West, he had been both willing and able to make this synthesis in his own life and prepare the stage for a synthesis on the cultural level. Merton said that Gandhi's success in synthesizing East and West in his own life led to his success in international politics, for he was indeed the only world figure of his day who seemed to be in control of himself, aware of other statesmen's feelings, and on top of events. Through his own successful synthesis he had received a vision of world unity, to be achieved through nonviolent protest of injustice, destruction, and genocide. Merton believed that the most significant product of Gandhi's successful life, that which grew out of his synthesis of East and West, that which made his life successful, was the philosophy of nonviolence.

Of course, Merton's admiration for Gandhi went deeper than his admiration for this particular philosophy. He was, in fact, attracted to him before he understood completely or espoused his teachings. One of the things he praised was Gandhi's personal integrity, as revealed by his refusal to recant his faith in nonviolence even when he saw his life's work being destroyed by India's division into two warring nations. He painted Gandhi in almost saintly colors when he described him as one who "never ceased to believe in the possibility of a love of truth so strong and so pure that it would leave an 'indelible impress' upon the most recalcitrant enemy, and awaken in him a response of love and truth." He even sketched Gandhi's death in terms which, were we to exchange "India" for "Israel," could easily sound like a description of the crucifixion of Christ: "But he himself recognized that politically his battle had really been lost. Without complacency, without self-pity, he faced the truth that there was only one thing left. He must lay down his life for India, and he was in fact killed by a brother 'whom he had failed to convince.' "[44]

To what extent Merton, because of his interest in and study of Asian religions, could see Gandhi as an Eastern epiphany of Christ is unknown (he did believe in the concept of Christ the Stranger), but it is obvious that he loved the man and his philosophy of nonviolence and did not hesitate to recommend them both to modern Christians for serious study. In his pre-Catholic days Merton followed Gandhi into pacifism; in the days of his monastic maturity he followed him into nonviolent protest. A philosophy which could make a "Christian" of a Hindu, he reasoned, might help make "Christians" of Christians.

Merton advised Christians to follow Gandhi both as an inspiration for faith and as a teacher of universal principles. He especially commended Gandhi's philosophy of nonviolent resistance to evil, which he believed provided the Christian with a strategy which could successfully attack and resolve modern problems. But he also pointed out several other important teachings and principles which, having grown naturally out of Gandhi's principle of nonviolence, were applicable to modern Christianity. Gandhi's belief that political activity and religious activity are one and the same, for example, could save the church from her ancient misconception about the absolute secularism of politics. Merton charged that the church, failing to see the spiritual significance of political acts and refusing to recognize the political gifts of many of her members, had estranged untold numbers of men whose idealism might have inspired them to play a creative role in political life. Many potential Christian statesmen, he said, had been pushed into parties "dominated by a confused pseudo-spirituality, or by totalitarian Messianism" because they were never told to pursue their political aspirations with the blessings of the church. For the Christian, Gandhi "remains in our time as a sign of the genuine union of spiritual fervor and social action in the midst of a hundred pseudo-spiritual crypto-fascist, or Communist movements of which the capacity for creative and spontaneous dedication is captured, debased and exploited by false prophets."[45]

Merton believed that Gandhi's principle of nonviolent resistance to evil, combined with his emphasis upon acts which were simultaneously religious and political, could be of immense benefit to any Christian who wanted to fulfill the commandments of Pope John's *Pacem in Terris*. The pope's call for Christians to work out their salvation in the world among men, Merton explained, would never be carried out by men who are exclusive, absolutist, or intolerant, nor by men who spout vague, liberal slogans and pious programs. They must be fulfilled by men who, because of inner synthesis and completeness, have found their "right mind."[46] Gandhi's philosophy, the result of such a man's experience, was perfectly suited to direct Christians to their right mind, to make them good Christians.

Merton believed that Gandhi could also teach modern Christians that all good political acts are manifestations of truth and that the achievement of truth is more significant than the success of the act, at least as the world counts success. Gandhi's acts were religious worship, he explained, acts to educate Indians in proper religious as well as political performance, and as such they were revelations of universal truth, designed to awaken men to the need for world unity.[47] Because Gandhi sought not security and strength for himself and his party alone but a new way of expressing the reality of the cosmos he was able to preserve his own integrity and inner peace, remaining detached from the results of his actions, which were thought to be in the hands of God anyway. He was able, because of his dedication to truth, to free himself and his acts from the inner violence of division and untruth, and for this reason his acts were essentially expressions of truth and consequently successful, always on the spiritual level and more often than not on the material.[48] Merton believed that if Christians would seek truth before political success they would not only please God but make more lasting contributions to the future of man.

He explained that Gandhi's philosophy of nonviolent resistance to evil would lead the Christian to active involvement in social reform rather than a passive evasion. He showed that Gandhi's nonviolent protest was no sentimental denial of the reality of evil; it was rather an acceptance of the need to use evil's power and presence "as a fulcrum for good and for liberation."[49] Gandhi faced every issue squarely, using his opponent's violence and power against him, and Merton argued that passive acquiescence to evil is the very anti-type of this approach. For Merton nonviolence was always positive and active, never negative and passive. He warned his readers not to dignify passive acquiescence by calling it nonviolence because it is actually pure cowardice, a parody of Christian nonviolence. He labeled as cowardice the passivism of Leopold Bloom in James Joyce's *Ulysses,* for it was nonviolence for the sake of fear rather than for the sake of conscience. If nonviolent resistance were impossible, Merton actually preferred force to passive acquiescence, and as a pattern for the nonviolent resister he pointed to Jesus' act of laying down his life for truth. Far from being an act of helpless passivity, as some modern writers like Nietzsche believed, Jesus' act was a "free and willing acceptance of suffering in the most positive and active manner."[50] Nonviolence, Merton concluded, "has been found wanting wherever it has been the non-violence of the weak. It has not been found so when it has been the non-violence of the strong."[51] Merton's philosophy would demand that its adherents march into a hostile, segregated neighborhood or resign a good job in a defense plant that makes nuclear weapons, both singularly difficult tasks.

But Merton pointed out that Gandhi would also teach Christians to be positive as well as strong, for the nonviolence of both Gandhi and Jesus presupposes that conditions can be improved. Thus Merton, who saw clearly the violent consequences of American and world folly, could believe that through nonviolent activities redemption might come. He explained as follows. Violent parties, such as the Nazis, believe that evil is irreversible and tend to become the most evil element in society in order to control society's evil; the nonviolent refuse to believe that evil conditions are irreversible and work to "change relationships that are evil into others that are good, or at least less bad." The violent, believing in the finality and omnipotence of evil, refuse to face the "precariousness and the risk that attend all finite good in this life"; the nonviolent believe that the fabric of society is unfinished, that it is constantly becoming and can be made better.[52] Merton's nonviolent acts were positive, constructive endeavors, tactics of love which tried to restore the basic unity of mankind by healing the divisions between men and reconciling the human family. They communicated love in acts rather than in words. Merton said that Gandhi had the wisdom of the Gospels when he taught his followers to overcome their enemies by loving them, by making them friends rather than enemies. Far from trying to humiliate the adversary, the nonviolent should seek to save him. Some who pretend to be nonviolent simply use nonviolence as a weapon to castigate, humiliate, and defeat their opponents, but Merton said "True nonviolence is totally different from this, and much more difficult. It strives to operate without hatred, without hostility, and without resentment. It works without aggression, taking the side of the good that it is able to find already present in the adversary."[53] Merton's nonviolent philosophy of social protest, based upon Gandhi's teachings, would make the enemy an object of love, thereby liberating both the oppressed and the oppressor of hate. True liberty, he once said, liberates both figures in the struggle. The oppressed man who gains liberty and immediately punishes or destroys his oppressor has merely initiated a new cycle of violence and oppression; the oppressed man who liberates both himself and his oppressor has truly gained the highest form of spiritual freedom and strength: strength of heart.

But to counter the charge that nonviolence is too idealistic, as this call for true liberty might well indicate, Merton pointed out that Gandhi's nonviolence makes its followers more realistic than adherents of most other social philosophies. He explained that Gandhi was not just pursuing a personal fantasy but was bravely expressing the unpopular but inescapable truth that a society whose politics are "violent, unreasonable, and inarticulate is sub-human" and must be condemned by reasonable men. Believing as all Hindus that all life is one, Gandhi condemned the caste system which paradoxically grew out of Hindu society but opposed it by dividing men and giving occasion to violence. Merton said that just as Gandhi opposed deeply rooted mores of his society so will any follower of nonviolence honestly admit the "inherent falsity and inner contradictions" of his own violent society and resist that violence nonviolently. He will bring the truth to his society even if he must suffer or die so that "injustice be unmasked and appear for what it really is."[54] This Merton did through his writings, and his criticism of American society in the 1960s brought him much criticism.

Finally, Merton believed that Gandhi's life and teaching could precipitate a kind of revival of spiritual devotion among reform-minded Christians by showing them that acts of charity and social concern must grow out of an inner strength, which he felt could best be found in contemplation. He explained that Gandhi's non-violence, which called for social unity and proved so effective in defending his people against their enemies, "sprang from an inner realization of spiritual unity in himself." Nonviolence in Merton's scheme was not therefore simply a political tactic which anyone can use to get what he wants, as it was not just a useful tool for Gandhi to use against the British; it was not a means of achieving unity so much as the "fruit of inner unity already achieved."[55] Before one goes into the world to resist evil through nonviolent protest, Merton said, he must discover this inner unity through contemplation.

Merton pointed out that all of Gandhi's teachings could be seen demonstrated in the work of Martin Luther King, Jr., and he advised his readers to listen to King and follow his Christian leadership in racial matters as well as Gandhi's teachings in world affairs. King's nonviolent protest marchers, combining religious zeal with political activity, were seeking the truth which would free their society from its racial curse. They realistically approached the evil of their society, calling upon an inner strength which some called soul power, a strength which indeed came from prayer.[56] Merton took his place beside Gandhi and King, believing that their philosophy was the only hope for man's dilemma, calling them the best examples of Christian witnesses in the modern world. Significantly, neither man shared Merton's Catholicism, and Gandhi was not even a Christian in the formal sense of the word.

Although he mourned the racial crisis and the questionable war, Merton did not despair of the world or America in the 1960s, for he discovered a redemptive philosophy and a few men who could make it work. Some of Merton's interpreters incorrectly took his warning against participating in the struggles of the earthly kingdoms to mean that Christians should withdraw and let the world go its own way. However, Merton was really saying, as the larger context of his writings proves, that Christians should try to remedy the world's ills without helping to create more, without contributing to its struggle for fame, wealth, or glory, and then to leave the results to God.[57] He explained: "We are living in the greatest revolution in history—a huge spontaneous upheaval of the entire human race: not the revolution planned and carried out by any particular party, race, or nation, but a deep elemental boiling over of all the inner contradictions that have ever been in man, a revelation of the chaotic forces inside everybody. This is not something we have chosen, nor is it something we are free to avoid."[58]

Because of his fame, Merton's later writings brought the message of the Indian Hindu and his black Baptist disciple to the attention of untold numbers of Roman Catholics, thus preparing the way for Catholic nonviolent resistance to injustice and war. He was not the only prominent Roman Catholic to espouse the philosophy of nonviolence, of course, but no other Catholic was so outspoken in his praise for Gandhi and King, so explicitly related nonviolence to the Gospels, used his prestige so unsparingly to bring the message of nonviolence to Catholics, and judging from the number of books and articles which he wrote on the subject had more effect on the Catholic community. Merton's own part in the peace and civil rights movements, because of his monastic vows, had to be inactive as well as nonviolent; he was forced to encourage such activities without himself being directly involved, but encourage them he did. He was forced to personify the unity that produces and results from nonviolence, to confine his participation to writing rather than acting.

But the question must be asked: Of what value will Merton's interpretations and teachings be in the 1970s and beyond, when the philosophy of nonviolence will presumably lose still more ground? His belief that a few people practicing nonviolence is as effective in solving the problems of the cold war and the racial crisis as the efforts of trained diplomats will obviously seem ridiculously idealistic to many people. His call for nonviolent protest against the violence of racial injustice and for Christians to resign good jobs in defense plants will perhaps sound not only impossible but unnecessarily old-fashioned to many in the next decade. He may even be accused of being an ivory-spire philosopher. But just because nonviolence is not momentarily in vogue its validity cannot be denied and its virtues forgotten. Because of his literary style Merton's writings will not be set aside, and when the eye-for-an-eye ethic that seems so popular presently is discredited, a new generation will look back to the nonviolence of Gandhi, King, and Merton. Surely the world needs a few men who can see the world's plight and formulate from their own authentic if limited experiences and reading a philosophy which can help solve the problems of society, a few idealists who believe that all good acts must be expressions of truth, who are able to call men back to primary principles, who see far beyond their own horizons, who are impractical but essential. Thomas Merton, the ivory-spire philosopher, was and through his writings will always be such a man.

Chapter Six

Catholicism in the Modern World

In the middle and late 1960s Thomas Merton's interest in the world focused ever more closely upon the relationship which he hoped would be established between the Roman Catholic Church and other Christian and even non-Christian religious bodies. The very circumstances of his death indicate the extent of his concern for ecumenical dialogue.

Although in the last fifteen years of his life he wrote on many different topics relating to the church and society, the main concern of his thinking and writing, from which all his other interests took their inspiration and direction, was to define his own role as a Catholic in the twentieth century. It was while trying to determine what a Catholic should be and do that his study of Christian history and thought led him to the study of other religions and theologies for clues to his own identity. He began to see that only in crossing borders of faith and confronting representatives of other religions could he hope to find himself and his own faith, and his participation in ecumenical dialogue, while rooted in his childhood Protestantism and a lifelong interest in Eastern thought, was nourished by his earnest desire to be an authentic person and a good churchman, a true Catholic in the modern world.

Merton came to believe, as he continued to study other religions and the deeper meaning of his own faith, that one is a true Catholic only if, in keeping with the traditional definition of the word, he is "universal" in understanding and sympathy, completely open to men with other viewpoints. Accordingly, he portrayed the true Catholic as one who is inclusive rather than exclusive, frank, honest, open, and willing to listen to men of all persuasions. The true Catholic, as Merton saw him, listens to the world as much as he speaks to it, is willing and able to discard old, dead ideas for new, live ones, and is constantly assimilating valuable teachings which come to him from the world into his faith, synthesizing truths from without with those already within, seeking to find a clearer expression and understanding of the revealed Word.[1] He said that to be open to other religious points of view was not to be indifferent to truth but to be committed to the inner reality of one's own doctrine rather than the doctrine itself. He admitted to his sorrow that Catholics have not always been willing to participate in ecumenical dialogue, that indeed many still are not, and that at times they have abandoned their own Catholic heritage and turned inward, rejecting all other philosophies as uninspired or even ungodly. He lamented the fact that many Catholics are still trying to live in what he called the era of Trent, those four hundred years from the Council of Trent to Vatican II, a time when Merton blamed the church for pretending to have God's final word in its final form. He heaped contempt upon the Trentian mentality, saying at one point that the "poor good people who have been paralyzed for ages by rigidities and conventions" are not really Catholics in the fullest sense of the word. He said, perhaps a bit too bluntly, that the stereotyped Catholic who lives by choice in an American Catholic ghetto, who is aggressive toward other faiths, rigid, limited, negative, and prejudiced, is precisely a non-Catholic. He felt that such people are unsuited for Christian witness in the modern world and often do more harm than good in the modern church.[2]

Because of his absence from American life during the 1940s and early 1950s, Merton was not as affected by the natural American tendency to mute religious beliefs in deference to national unity as were most Catholics after World War II. His own independently expanding awareness of non-Catholic practices and thought was more influenced and encouraged by the Second Vatican Council, which he praised as the most significant event of modern church history. The solitary Trappist wrote that Pope John's desire to draw the Roman church closer to the churches of Greece, Russia, and the Orient, as manifest in the Council, had started a truly

Catholic movement within a church which called itself Catholic but was not really so. Caring more about people than institutions, Pope John was teaching Catholics the value of confronting and seeking to understand men of other faiths, and Merton encouraged all his brethren to become true Catholics by following the pope's example. He was obviously delighted that the Council was breaking up the icy influence of Trent, and he wrote long letters to the American delegates, suggesting possible new approaches and congratulating them for making it possible for Catholics to receive as well as to give out the truth.[3] While the Council did not give birth to Merton's ecumenical spirit, it did motivate, sustain, and give legitimacy to a spirit that was already there.

Merton sincerely hoped that the Council would effectively return the church to the pathway of openness from which it had strayed since the catastrophe of the Protestant Reformation. His study of church history led him to believe that until the Council of Trent (he probably should have set the date earlier) the church was the Great Synthesizer, listening to various non-Christian thinkers and writers and incorporating their most valuable teachings into Christian theology. He cited three examples. The early church fathers were quick to see the value of classical Greek Humanism and through synthesis, illustrated by Augustine's synthesis of Christianity and neo-Platonism, produced some of Christianity's most effective and long-lasting doctrines. Medieval Scholastic philosophers combined their received dogma with the newly rediscovered Greek, Roman, and Arabic manuscripts to create some of the church's most intelligent and soaring statements of faith, as illustrated by Saint Thomas's synthesis of Christianity with Aristotelianism. Early Jesuit missionaries to China, seeking the salvation of the Chinese and seeing the remarkable similarities between the writings of Confucius and Saint Benedict, collected and translated large numbers of oriental texts, paving the way for a possible synthesis of Christian and Confucian thought, a synthesis which was never realized due to the closed, non-Catholic attitude of their contemporaries. Merton believed that the first two instances of synthesis gave Catholics deeper insight into their own faith, strengthened the church's theological system, and proved that those who bear the name of Christ can find expression for their faith anywhere on earth.[4] He sorrowed over the failure of the Jesuits to synthesize Christianity with an Eastern philosophy, and in a sense Merton's own later writings attempted to do just that.

The liberated Merton of the 1960s reminded his Catholic readers that it was within the context of their faith that the medieval concept of Christ the Stranger gained its greatest adherence. He explained that Christians in the Middle Ages were taught to show hospitality to strangers because, as Jesus had warned, a stranger might be either Christ himself or one of his messengers. Here again he blamed the upheavals of the sixteenth century for destroying the true Catholic spirit, for after the Protestant Reformation Catholics began to show hospitality only to their own kind. He warned that if the church did not return to this important heritage it might well be unprepared for the appearance of Christ as a stranger. He explained: "It is true that the visible Church alone has the official mission to sanctify and teach all nations, but no one knows that the stranger he meets coming out of the forest in a new country is not already an invisible member of Christ and perhaps one who has some providential or prophetic message to utter."[5]

He also called his readers' attention to western man's traditional love of pilgrimages, a tradition which from the earliest days of Christianity has encouraged the followers of Jesus to travel long and short distances to shrines in search of deeper meaning for life. The first crusade, which triggered European conquest of most of the world within six hundred years of its beginning, was in large measure a reaction to the Turkish decree that no Christians be allowed to make pilgrimages to the Holy Land, and even the mass immigration to America was seen by many of its participants as a pilgrimage to a new land of God's own making. Perhaps Merton was historically and psychologically correct to remind Catholics that the pilgrimage is western man's most distinctive characteristic and to teach modern Catholics that their own pilgrimage should be to the strange lands of other religions and philosophies in search of the deeper truths of Christianity.[6] Because of his prestige many Catholics listened when Merton spoke such words, words which other churchmen might have spoken earlier but with less effect.

Merton was himself a true Catholic, but he admitted that it was only in the last few years of his life that he became one. In the early days of his profession of faith, the days so well described in

The Seven Storey Mountain, he felt that the church possessed ultimate and sacred truth, that it held in trust the final revelation of God in Christ, and that it must call the world to itself for salvation. In those days he rejected the world outside the church and had no apparent interest in establishing dialogue with it. But upon his emergence from the enforced silence of the 1940s he began to listen as well as speak to the world and to make friends with many of the world's citizens, and much later he would say that it was only then that he became a true Catholic.

One example of his conversion to openness may be seen in a letter to a rabbi who had written to Merton about a reference in *The New Man* to the Suffering Servant's being both Israel and Christ. Merton observed that Christianity and Judaism are much closer in spirit and thought than either has ever been willing to admit and that the two faiths should look for their common ideals in an effort to find the ultimate truth which they both possess in different forms. In another letter, this one to a Muslim, Merton emphasized the utmost importance of mutual comprehension between Christians and Muslims, and he suggested that during their holy seasons they pray for each other and for more dialogue between their peoples.[7] Such examples are abundant in Merton's files.

Merton also took every available opportunity during the second half of his career to establish dialogue with the so-called unbeliever, as illustrated by an article entitled "How It Is—Apologies to an Unbeliever," published in *Harper's Magazine* in 1967. Using a tone which at times seemed a bit too chummy but which was obviously sincere, he apologized for the embarrassing and false attitude of some believers toward the people whom they label unbelievers. He explained that sometimes the believer is himself really the unbeliever, for he tends to trust his religious institution more than God, and that sometimes the unbeliever is actually the believer, for he believes in truth enough to say honestly that the theological jargon of the church makes no sense to him. Merton said that the true nonbeliever, which he thought was a more accurate term than unbeliever, is usually more religious than the overt believer because even without the trappings of formal religion he is often closer to the ground of his own being, which is God. In conclusion, he pointed with some pride to Vatican II's suggestion that Christians begin to listen to the nonbeliever rather than simply condemn him. Merton believed that things were at least taking a turn for the better.[8]

Merton's appeal brought warm response from many thoughtful unbelievers who themselves welcomed dialogue with this brilliant and open-minded Catholic. Merton was even able to establish dialogue with many advocates of philosophies which were thought by some to be alien to Christian theology. When criticized for his strange bedfellows he answered that Christian theology has often in the past benefited from its association with philosophies which, had they been rejected out of hand as some churchmen wanted him to reject modern secular philosophies, might have destroyed it or robbed it of some valuable insights. He pointed out that existentialism, which originally began in Christian circles and was best expressed in the nineteenth century by the Danish Protestant Soren Kierkegaard, was a definite threat to Christianity in the 1940s because of its recently acquired atheism. At that time some Christian theologians were saying that one must be either a Christian or an existentialist, and Merton believed that had that attitude prevailed Christianity might have lost some of its most brilliant young thinkers, and the valuable teachings of existentialism might have been lost as its atheism pulled it into oblivion. He was therefore pleased that some Christians, seeing the truths to be gained from existentialism, had read the works of the existentialists and had incorporated them into Christian theology, thereby creating Christian existentialism in which the "blank, godless nothingness of freedom and of the person, Sartre's *neant,* becomes the luminous abyss of divine gift." This synthesis, which he explained might not have occurred had Christians been afraid to establish dialogue, gave to Christianity some new and some long-neglected emphases, such as a better analysis of man's nature and the condition of his existence, a strong emphasis upon man's freedom, and a challenge to the sterility and inner hopelessness of modern life, the "negative cult of life-denying despair" so popular in our day.[9] Merton himself was vitally interested in existentialism, which he believed to be the most important secular philosophy of the twentieth century, and several of his later articles and booklets dealt with the philosophy of the great French existentialist Albert Camus.

The dialogue which caused some of Merton's fellow Catholics the most embarrassment was his friendship with Marxists. When criticized for this interest he explained that Marxism, which is indeed a form of religion, contains definite "inner spiritual potentials" and "genuine pretensions to humanism" which are often hidden beneath its repugnant dialectical dogma. Christianity agrees with Marxism, he said, that man must break free from his subordination to machines and the entire technological process, gain control over them, break the chains of his alienation, and become the master of his own history. Dialogue between Christianity and Marxism was not only possible but necessary, for each could help to correct the other's faults, and so Merton called for more interaction between progressive Catholic thinkers of the West and revisionist Marxists of the East.[10]

Perhaps most significant for the American scene was Merton's dialogue with Protestantism. He corresponded and talked personally with many Protestants, mostly those who themselves were open enough to talk freely with a Catholic monk, and out of this dialogue came ideas which were helpful to both Catholics and Protestants. During his years of dialogue with them, Protestant theologians, influenced by the thinking of the martyred Lutheran pastor Dietrich Bonhoeffer, were placing more and more emphasis upon the secularization of Christianity, and Merton responded to this movement with interest and enthusiasm. He was particularly intrigued and at times amazed by the book *Honest to God* by the Anglican bishop John A. T. Robinson, the first ranking member of the Anglican hierarchy to try speaking to modern secular man in his own language and style.[11] The ideas in this book were for the most part borrowed from such prominent theologians as Bonhoeffer, Paul Tillich, and Rudolf Bultmann and thus represented the more creative Protestant thought of the twentieth century, and because they were presented in layman's language by no less than a bishop they were given a wide reading by both Catholics and Protestants.

Robinson addressed himself ostensibly to modern man, who he said can no longer believe in the old image of the God-out-There. He suggested that the church give up its privileged position and become simply man's servant, talking no longer of God and speaking of Jesus simply as "the man for others." All this, he said, would be more honest to God. Merton admitted that Protestants are in general freer to pursue this type of thought than most Catholics, but he felt that perhaps their freedom had led them to some serious errors. He said that if men like Bishop Robinson had been better grounded in the traditional Christian writers such as the Latin fathers, Thomas Aquinas, and John of the Cross they would not have walked into such confusion. But he admired their daring attempt to speak to modern man, and he rebuffed those who questioned their Christianity by recalling that the "religionless" Bonhoeffer died for his faith while many church Christians lined up to march in the ungodly Nazi parades.

While he admired Bishop Robinson's attempt to speak to contemporary man and was probably influenced by him to do likewise, he seemed genuinely surprised that a theologian like Robinson had so late in life come to understand or say publicly that no mythical or poetic symbol is adequate to describe God. He wondered in fact whether Robinson even yet fully understood that no concept is adequate for God, for *Honest to God* seemed to him to be devising new symbols which would themselves soon be dated and thus inadequate. Merton suggested to the Protestants that Christians try to get along with no symbol at all, just referring to God as inexpressible reality, for all symbols finally deny his transcendence. He said that while Robinson warned against conditioning the unconditioned he was busy reconditioning the unconditioned.

He also criticized Robinson's attempt to modify the image of Christianity, not because he went too far but because he did not go far enough. He agreed with Robinson that the present image of Christianity is inadequate for the modern world and that perhaps Christians should try to get along with no conscious image at all, but he protested that Robinson, far from stripping the modern Christian of an image, had actually tried to give him a reconditioned image: the image of a man free of mythology, well-read in existentialism, and able to practice the new morality without guilt. Since the Christian gospel demands that Christians deny the world at some point, Merton suggested that it be at the point of misrepresenting themselves. He believed that Christians should be contemporary men who also happen to be children of God through Christ, not old-fashioned men stripped of their myths and clothed in new ones whose relevance will last for only a short time. The ambiguity of Robinson's modern Christian, Merton concluded, makes him both ineffectual and ridiculous.

Just before his fatal pilgrimage to the East, Merton told me that the theologians who run along after the world yelling "Look! We're relevant!" have virtually no influence upon the very type of person they are trying to reach: modern, secular man. He believed that the only person helped by Robinson's type of theology is the Christian who is already committed to the church but whose faith has been shaken by life in the modern world. He alone will be encouraged by a bishop who admits that stale theology is at best relative and at worst demonic, for he alone has given it that much thought. Merton saw great value in the book and the theology that it represented, but he warned that it is only for believers; unbelievers will never read it, or if they do it will simply confirm what they have known all along: that Christianity is irrelevant. Merton in fact believed that Robinson had destroyed his opportunity to communicate with modern, secular man by abdicating his theological position, thus having nothing to say to him. By preaching that the Christian should abandon "religion" and plunge into an apparently "godless secularism out of love for God's world and of the people in it," he had told modern, secular man that God wants him to live without him—something that modern, secular man already knows and does. Merton's criticism might be summed up in these words written during the last year of his life: "I think that *Honest to God* is an expression of sincere but misdirected concern: a concern to find 'fellowship' with modern secular man on a level that is still ambiguous and superficial because it still attempts, though with all decency and much tact, to 'sell' a reconditioned image of a Christianity that is 'worldly,' 'religionless' and free of myths. This may be all very well, but the unconditional character of the Christian concern, to use the Bishop's own language, demands that at some point one confront 'the world' with a refusal. We know, in fact, that Bonhoeffer did just this."[12]

Merton responded just as enthusiastically yet ambiguously to two other expressions of Protestant thought in the 1960s: the secular-city movement, begun by Harvey Cox, and the death-of-God movement, begun by a group of men which included Thomas Altizer, William Hamilton, and Gabriel Vahanian. While he applauded both attempts to reach modern man, he felt that their abdication of God would inevitably force them into the arms of a demonic society. To praise the secular city in which man lives, he warned, could lead to the worship of American affluence, the military-industrial complex, and the war in Vietnam, although nothing could be farther from these authors' minds. He believed that to confess that God does not exist in our society could easily lead to a celebration of the state as God's successor and then to passive or even worshipful acquiescence to totalitarian dictatorship. While Merton was in sympathy with the spirit of such movements, he felt that their intellectual expressions were wrong, perhaps demonstrating that the intellectual wall between Catholicism and Protestantism is thicker and higher than many ecumenists would like to admit.[13] But Merton kept trying to scale that wall.

Although he saw many flaws in the various Protestant movements toward relevance and secularity, Merton praised them for trying to speak to modern man in his own language and was pleased that Vatican II was attempting to do likewise. While he warned the church not to abdicate its theological position by denying the reality of God or the redemption of Christ, he did think that it should prepare for its inevitable minority status, the diaspora which was sure to come in the near future. He said that Christians should be prepared to discuss, explain, and share their faith with those who have no faith, not in order to prove themselves right or to appear fashionable to twentieth-century man, but out of thanks to God for his grace. The diaspora, which would have no established church and few Christians, would call for Christians who believe in their own tradition but who recognize the mythical character of its terminology and who are open to discuss it frankly with anyone who might be interested. For Merton Christianity was not a matter of choosing either God or man but of "finding God by loving man, and discovering the true meaning of man in our love for God."[14]

Merton's article "How It Is—Apologies to an Unbeliever" might appear to be an honest-to-God attempt to speak to modern man, and some might accuse him of "selling out" to make himself relevant. But there is one difference. He apologized not for the Christian message but for the actions and attitudes of Christians, or people who call themselves Christians. For Merton the message is essentially the same forever, requiring constant reinterpretation and synthesis with other serious thought, but it cannot be cast aside for the ill-defined and sometimes ungodly thought of the secular world. The Christian must love his fellowman and respond to his attempt to find meaning in life; he must not abdicate his own reason for existence. Although he encouraged the renewal of the church and his order as inspired by Pope John XXIII, his later writings, especially his speeches on the trip to Bangkok, indicate a growing disillusionment with renewal in the late 1960s. He felt that renewal had become a fad and had lost its authenticity. Many churchmen were reforming for reform's sake, destroying the valid practices with the invalid, stripping the church of its true heritage and legitimate values. And, to be honest, it must be admitted that Merton seemed sometimes to espouse certain causes because they were unpopular, or at least unespoused within the church, only to become disenchanted with them when they became common causes. Such was the case with renewal and seemed to be the case also with certain types of civil rights activists and peace maneuverers. Yet he was a progressive, and in his defense we must remember these words, written in 1965: "The extreme progressives [at the Council] seem to me, as far as I can judge with the poverty of my information, to be hasty, irresponsible, in many ways quite frivolous in their exaggerated and confused enthusiasms. They also seem to me at times to be fanatically incoherent, but I do not sense in them the chilling malice and meanness which comes through in some of the utterances of extreme conservatives."[15]

During the latter years of his life, as he took more seriously the responsibility of presenting Christianity's message to the world in a relevant way and as he looked more favorably upon other philosophies which might give it strength and clarification, Merton became ever more interested in Asia and her religions. While a student in England in the early 1930s he had studied the teachings and activities of Mahatma Gandhi, and his acquaintance with the Hindu monk Bramachari at Columbia again whetted his appetite for Eastern thought. With his expanded freedom in the late 1950s and 1960s, he renewed this interest and became something of an authority on Eastern religions. He came to believe that the survival of mankind depended upon a synthesis of Eastern and Western cultures and that the histories and philosophies of India, Japan, and China should be studied alongside those of Greece and Rome in American universities. He shocked some Catholics by bluntly saying that Christianity needs oriental religious thought. He explained that because it is a supernatural religion Christianity does not need further fulfillment but that it does need the enrichment that oriental religions can give it. Because Christianity, the Great Synthesizer, had in its better moments listened to other religions and incorporated their messages into itself, thereby retaining and strengthening its catholicity, Merton encouraged Christians to study the great oriental religions which were available to them and to tap their rich resources. He practiced what he preached.[16]

He reacted angrily to the rather common theory that Christianity should conquer and subdue other religions rather than establish dialogue with them. He deplored Roman Catholic practices in the Americas during the sixteenth century, when the cross followed the cannon, when missionaries planted the Christian flag of Spain on the burning rubble of Mexican culture, but he pointed with pride to the work of the early Jesuits in China during the same period. In his book *Mystics and Zen Masters* he told the story of these first Jesuit missionaries to China who developed an appreciation for Confucianism, adopted the scholarly robes and methods of Chinese teachers, and tried to synthesize Christianity and Confucianism so that the Chinese might experience the best of both religions.[17] But other Catholic missionaries, who were denied entrance to China for some time and thus had no idea what their more fortunate colleagues were experiencing, began to accuse them of apostasy. Confusing Confucianism with some form of idolatry, these ill-informed priests on the outside reported that the Jesuits had converted to a pagan religion and abandoned Christianity. Merton showed great contempt for the "orthodox" Catholics who, like their counterparts in sixteenth- and twentieth-century America, acted in an ignorant and totally uncatholic manner. He praised the early Jesuit missionaries in China, explaining that their willingness to set aside their own culture for the sake of the gospel and their fellowman made them true missionaries and good examples for modern Catholics to emulate. By responding to the best elements of Confucianism and sacrificing the "Italian" elements of Christianity while retaining Christ and the Sacraments, they created a faith that was relevant for the Chinese and established a pattern for the modern Catholic to follow.

By the early eighteenth century the Jesuits in China had written Chinese rites for the Chinese people who wished to become Christians. These rites permitted the Chinese to retain the Confucian philosophy of life and such cultural mores as the honoring of ancestors even after becoming Christians. It was a nearly perfect synthesis. But the dissident priests focused so much attention and criticism upon the Chinese rites that the pope banned them, and they remained illegal for two centuries. When the ban was finally lifted in 1939 China refused to accept Christian missionaries, and the great opportunity was lost. Merton concluded that the blindness which destroyed the Christian witness in China would neutralize the power of Christ in every age and on every continent unless men of concern and love first brought light to their own people before going out to meet the non-Christian. And so he approached the representatives of Eastern religions as a brother, making it plain that he needed them as much as they needed him, all the while explaining in books and articles and poems what he was doing so that Catholics would understand and participate in his grand experiment. At times this took great patience.

Merton pointed to the first Jesuit missionaries to China as an example for the modern Catholic, for he believed that in their honesty and daring they were three hundred years ahead of their time, fulfilling the obligations of the twentieth century in the sixteenth. He explained that just as the apostle Paul used one approach when preaching in Athens and the apostle Peter used another in Jerusalem so should Catholics today use different approaches to different cultures, fitting the method to the circumstances; just as the early Christians opposed the vices of Greece and Rome but adopted their language, philosophical expressions, and architecture so should Catholics today borrow the philosophical and stylistic expressions of the Orient; just as the Jesuits in China, because of their openness, accepted the brief epiphany of the Son of Man as a Chinese scholar so should modern Catholics honestly search for whatever epiphany God chooses today.

Encouraged by Vatican II's statement that while the church believes Jesus Christ to be God's most definitive expression it rejects nothing good or holy in any other faith, Merton began to look for the good in other faiths and as time went by more and more in the religious wisdom of the Orient. He felt a personal and vocational responsibility to enter into dialogue with Eastern theologians because through his reading and thinking he came to believe that the most fruitful and rewarding level of ecumenical exchange would be carried on by the contemplatives of the Orient and Occident. While the obstacles to dialogue on the doctrinal level might be insurmountable, it would be possible to discuss openly and frankly the disciplines and rewards of the contemplative life, which is basically the same in all religions, and from that to move to even more important subjects. Zen Buddhist monks and Christian Cistercians, he explained, because they are so similar in their simplicity, austerity, uncompromising poverty, manual labor, and common life, would be able to understand each other more easily than Buddhist and Christian theologians.[18] And so Merton began, through his personal activities and writings, to establish dialogue with Eastern thinkers, especially monks. He hoped that by his example he might lead other Catholics to confront the Orient, learn to appreciate its rich heritage, and begin to think beyond their religion to the larger religious family of man. He wrote in his Asian journal that he hoped to find on his trip "the great solution," which probably meant the true religious synthesis that he always believed both possible and desirable.

One result of Merton's involvement with Eastern religious thought was a circle of new friends who added to his knowledge of the Orient and of mankind in general. One of the most significant of these friends, from whom he derived his attitude toward the war in Vietnam, was the controversial Vietnamese Zen Buddhist Nhat Hanh, who visited Merton at Gethsemani during his trip to the United States in 1966. An article which Merton wrote after this visit, called "Nhat Hanh Is My Brother," demonstrated his ability to relate with men of other faiths, especially Eastern faiths. He explained that he and Nhat Hanh were brothers because they saw things alike; they both deplored the war that was ravaging Vietnam, opposing it for "human reasons, reasons of sanity, justice and love." Merton was pleased to see the warm reception Hahn had received from the American public, which he said is usually so ill-informed by its mass media, for it proved to him that Americans were still searching for truth and could still decide in favor of a man and against a political machine when given the chance. He feared for Nhat Hanh's life when he returned to Vietnam, knowing that he would likely be imprisoned, tortured, and/or killed for his support of the Vietnamese people against the established government, the militant Buddhists, the Viet Cong, and the North Vietnamese Communist government. He explained that he had more in common with Nhat Hanh than with most Americans, for the bonds that united them were "the bonds of a new solidarity and a new brotherhood which is beginning to be evident on all the five continents and which cuts across all political, religious, and cultural lines to unite young men and women in every country in something that is more concrete than an ideal and more alive than a program. This unity of the young is the only hope of the world."[19]

Merton's interest in contemporary Eastern philosophy led him to dig deeply into the Orient's past in search of more enlightenment. One by-product of this quest was his book *The Way of Chuang Tzu,* a poetic paraphrase of selected writings of Chuang Tzu, a third century B.C. Chinese philosopher and the chief spokesman of all times for Taoism.[20] Using translations already available in English, he organized and rephrased them so as to let them speak to the concerns and problems of modern Christians. Throughout the book the reader is made aware of the striking similarities of Chuang Tzu's thought to that of Cistercian Christianity, and even allowing for Merton's own bias in selecting the passages the similarities are too numerous and obvious to be fabrications. He actually proved that Chuang Tzu could be used to teach truths which some might have believed lay within the domain of Christianity alone. For example, in one section Chuang Tzu discusses the wisdom of being considered useless by society, a theme found in many of Merton's own writings. Chuang Tzu says that useful trees, such as the Cinnamon, are cut down and their lives ended early but that the useless tree is left alone to live in the sun until its natural time to die. And yet "No one seems to know / How useful it is to be useless." And so Chuang Tzu teaches the importance of being "useless" in the eyes of the world, a theme that seems to be universal since it also runs all through Western contemplative literature.

In another passage the emperor sends a messenger to ask Chuang Tzu to be his prime minister, but Chuang Tzu prefers to be a simple philosopher and so tells the messenger a parable of two turtles: one a sacred turtle who lives in the temple and stays forever on the altar; the other a common turtle who drags his tail in the mud all day. Chuang Tzu then asks the emperor's messenger which of the turtles lives the better life, the one who is honored or the one who does what is natural to him, and when the messenger answers the latter:

> "Go home!" said Chuang Tzu.
> "Leave me here
> To drag my tail in the mud!"

One can almost hear Merton saying these same words to those who wanted him to leave the monastery and receive the honor his literary achievements deserved. And it is certainly in accord with Merton's view of Christianity that Chuang Tzu says: "Great knowledge sees all in one. / Small knowledge breaks down into the many."

Merton was puzzled and a bit disgusted to find that some of his fellow Catholics criticized his study of Eastern religions and accused him of unholy syncretism. He defended his right to read and discuss the writing of such great philosophers as Chuang Tzu by appealing once again to the history of Christian theology. "If St. Augustine could read Plotinus, if St. Thomas could read Aristotle and Averroes (both of them certainly a long way further from Christianity than Chuang Tzu ever was!), and if Teilhard de Chardin could make copious use of Marx and Engels in his synthesis, I think I may be pardoned for consorting with a Chinese recluse who shares the climate and peace of my own kind of solitude, and who is my own kind of person."[21]

Merton found his study of individual oriental philosophers, both modern and ancient, so beneficial that he began to study whole systems of Eastern thought during the last few years of his life. He studied Taoism, came to appreciate its wisdom, and concluded that if given the chance it could add many new things to Christianity and revive many old and half-forgotten but still valuable teachings already within Christian thought. For example, he believed that Taoism, because of its emphasis upon the contemplative life, could help Christianity reaffirm its need for contemplation. He explained that Taoism's founder Lao Tzu, fearing systematic theology and Confucius' attempt to collect and preserve sacred Chinese writings, envisioned a monastic society in the form of a small primitive community, a few villages inhabited by selfless men living in harmony with the hidden, ineffable Tao. Lao Tzu's vision became the foundation stone of Taoism. The secret of life which these men would seek could be found within themselves, not through an intellectual quest for knowledge or power but through the contemplative act of walking the Tao or Way. According to

Lao Tzu, the one who discovered the secret of life would not be hyperactive or possess esoteric knowledge that set him apart from other men; he would in fact be less remarkable than other men. He would be a contemplative. Merton believed that if Catholics could ever come to appreciate the role which such a man played in Taoism they would appreciate more the role of their own contemplatives.

Merton also suggested that Christians observe and benefit from their study of the Taoist pattern for the family. Admitting that Lao Tzu's social system was adequate only for a few contemplatives and not for society as a whole, he believed that Taoist ideals concerning family life were valid for all societies and might well serve as a corrective for the social chaos of modern America. He explained that the Taoist teachings about filial love, contrary to Western man's mistaken impression, do not encourage a suffocating ancestor worship but call for a true and complete development of the whole person; one's parents give him his personhood, and he shows his respect for them by developing his personhood and by caring for them in their old age. In his life within the family each person observes and develops the five important character traits which he will need in life: the father shows justice to his son; the mother shows compassion and merciful love to her son; the son shows filial love to his parents; the elder brother shows friendship to his younger brother; and the younger brother shows respect to his elder brother. The family thus helps the individual to develop the necessary characteristics of strength, warmth, gratitude, and respectful friendship. The man who develops his personhood in this way will not be too proud in a high station, will not be too insubordinate in an inferior station, and will be conscientious among equals.[22]

Another strain of Eastern thought which attracted Merton's attention and captured his imagination was the Ju school of thought, founded by Kung Tzu (Confucius) and later refined and expanded by Meng Tzu (Mencius). Merton approved of their emphasis upon education and intellectual development, which he admitted was a healthy antidote to Lao Tzu's anti-intellectualism, but most of all he admired their emphasis upon the basic goodness of man, which the Ju philosophers said would blossom if cultivated by a just society. Merton believed that Confucianism could help the Christian regain his faith in the goodness of man and inspire him to establish a just society with just rulers who by their rule would expose the good that is naturally within man.

To illustrate the Ju school's view of human nature and society, Merton published a translation and interpretation of Meng Tzu's "Ox Mountain Parable," which tells of a village whose residents cut the trees from a wooded hill and let their sheep graze upon the sprouts, keeping the hill so completely smooth that no one who passed would believe it had ever been wooded. The parable means, Merton explained, that while a bad society may destroy man's natural goodness to such an extent that no one will believe it good at all, the restoration of a proper political and social climate, like the abolition of grazing sheep, will permit the goodness to grow again. Following the teachings of the Ju school, Merton argued that the primary task of social leaders is to bring out man's natural goodness by providing facilities for educating his followers in humaneness. Men who are properly educated recapture the heart of a child, the deep and spontaneous instinct for love; they develop their "night spirit," their unconscious nature that leads them to good acts, the product of their "right mind."[23] Thus Merton took the side of Confucius against such Christian thinkers as Machiavelli and John Calvin, who asserted that man is not naturally good.

But more important among Eastern philosophies and religions than either Taoism or Confucianism for Merton was Zen Buddhism, which he believed contained certain universal truths that the passage of time and the demands of a new age have not and cannot diminish. He said that Zen, which is more a method than a formal religion, could be helpful to modern man as he seeks meaning in life and particularly to the modern Christian as he seeks to increase the scope and depth of his faith. Merton recommended that Christians observe Zen discipline, which helps one overcome his attachment to individual self-affirmation and survival, the source of man's sorrows. Since their faith teaches them a life of selfless service, Christians could find in Zen exercises a means of fulfilling the demands of their own religion.

Merton explained that when Buddha said, "Be lamps for yourselves," he was not equating the "self" with the empirical "I." He was saying rather that in order to be a lamp to himself a man must die to "I" and submit himself to an enlightened teacher who will lead him in turn to enlightenment. The enlightened teacher gives the student a *koan,* which is usually a meaningless sentence, and tells him to work for a logical interpretation. For months his every report is rejected by the teacher, and only after as much as a year of frustration and disappointment he finally learns the hard lesson that the *koan* cannot be interpreted intellectually and that he himself is a *koan,* a riddle with no answer that can be communicated objectively.[24] By teaching the student that he is basically unintelligible, the sage liberates him from his self-consciousness, delivering him from himself.

Not only liberation from self but a renewed emphasis upon a positive response to life could result from a Christian studying Zen, Merton believed. By responding directly to the *koan* the student learns to respond directly to life, which is also a riddle with no intelligible answer. The teacher does not want a clever or even a correct answer but a living and authentic response to life as symbolized by the *koan.* The student who can respond directly and immediately to the *koan* is believed capable of responding fully, directly, and immediately to life itself. The *koan* reminded Merton of primitive cave art which "neither represents the object nor expresses the reaction of the subject" but "celebrates the *act of seeing* as a holy and transcendent discovery." Believing that Christianity has too often in the past turned from life in the name of Jesus Christ, Merton suggested that Zen's emphasis upon this response to life might be a corrective both for the typical Christian assumption that the puzzle of life is easy to solve and for the typical Christian refusal to respond to life as it is.[25]

According to a growing legend, a man came to Gethsemani and poured out a long tale of woe to Merton, who sat silently listening until the end when he responded to the man's problems with a one-word solution: live. This answer indicates no lack of concern, although it might well reveal an awareness of his own limitations in advising men about their problems. It is a Christian answer, clarified by Merton's study of Zen, a universal answer, an appropriate answer for modern man. How this admonition is to be applied must be determined by each man in his freedom, but the admonition rings true.

Merton believed that Zen's emphasis upon experience would help to liberate Christians from their slavery to dogma. Buddhism, which places experience at the heart of religious faith and regards doctrinal formulations as relatively unimportant, could remind the

Christian not to neglect the experience of his faith while concentrating solely upon doctrine. Merton acknowledged the validity of tending to theological statements, their accurate transmission, their precise meanings, and the elimination of errors in their presentation, all of these being traditional Christian concerns, but he warned that this concern could become an obsession and make the Christian forget that Christianity is essentially a "living experience of unity in Christ which far transcends all conceptual formulations." Merton always believed that in dialogue with Zen the Christian would recapture and reaffirm the experiential nature of his faith.

And he believed that Zen could teach Christians better understanding of contemplation. Zen masters neither affirm nor deny anything, and enlightenment comes neither by quietistic inactivity or by self-conscious overactivity, for both attitudes tend to make the person a subject and all others objects, creating a false and dangerous dichotomy. Enlightenment in Zen is not a vision of Buddha or an I-Thou relationship with a Supreme Being, for the teacher neither affirms nor denies the existence of Buddha or even God. Enlightenment is rather "the ontological *awareness of pure being beyond subject and object,* an immediate grasp of being in its 'suchness' and 'thusness.'" Merton explained that this ideal could be found in the Christian concept of contemplation, in which the dichotomies between God and man and between man and man are dissolved, and that perhaps through a study of Zen the Christian could rediscover this most important part of his own heritage.[26]

Merton advised Christians to study Zen and thereby rediscover their own faith in its purest form. He said that Zen is compatible with Christianity because it helps its followers find direct experience on the "metaphysical level, liberated from verbal formulas and linguistic preconceptions." He explained: "It refuses to make a claim to any special revelation or to a mystical light, and yet if it is followed on, in line with its own vast and open perspectives, it is certainly compatible with a revelation of inscrutable freedom, love, and grace."[27]

Merton's great fear was that Eastern religious thought would soon be closed to the West. Hoping that the religious thought of the East would have a future in Western Christian lands, he pleaded with his readers to learn as much as possible about Eastern thought and culture before the Communists rebuild the Orient into a blurred copy of the industrialized West, replacing the rich

Eastern heritage with a spiritual poverty like our own. He hoped that by a synthesis of East and West the world would regain its sight and move into a new day of wisdom and progress.[28]

Merton's openness reflected the attitude of his church's greatest thinkers in the 1960s, and his writings brought this attitude to the attention of countless Catholics, both clergy and laity, who were able to understand, appreciate, and even adopt his attitude toward Eastern religions. The extent of his influence upon ecumenism is incalculable, but the very number of people who read his articles and books on the subject of religious synthesis was enormous. His sincerity, his literary skill, and the great following he had amassed in the earlier, simpler days made him a powerful voice for ecumenism, and death has not stilled that voice.

And so the thread that runs through all Merton's works, from the early poetry through his "spiritual" writings to the social and ecumenical teachings of the 1960s, is this theme of unity: unity of man with God and of man with man. As a young man Merton abandoned the world of disunity, spent more than ten years separated from it in cloistered isolation, and then with a burst of creative energy again faced that world and sought to prescribe remedies for its fragmentation. When he entered the monastery, he was running away from a world which he saw as tragically fragmented and hopelessly at odds with itself. Having been a sensitive citizen of that world, he shared its fragmentation, and his own inner disunity, which either mirrored or helped create this corporate fragmentation, drove him in his distraction to the monastery. However, because his years at Gethsemani enabled him to gain personal inner unity, he could begin to dream of a society also unified through contemplation of God, and his last years were dedicated to fulfilling this dream.

He was an intensely personal writer, always seeking through his early poetry and novels, his later meditations on the contemplative life, and his late social commentaries to understand himself as well as the world, and he always saw the world as a macrocosm of Thomas Merton. Thus what had happened in his own experience, he reasoned, could happen to the world. The world which he rediscovered in the 1950s was as fragmented as it had been in the 1930s, but Merton the observer had changed. The warring factions within him were for the most part reconciled, and he had found union with God and with his fellowman through contemplation, and he could now try to bring about unity within man's society. The society which Merton had rejected was one in which he had played an extremely unhappy role; the society which he later came to love was a society in which he could, because he had made peace with God and himself, play a creative role. Seeing man's society as a torn cloth, divided into nations, races, religions, and ideologies, he preached that until these divisions were healed, until the cloth were mended, the danger of destruction was imminent. The entire last decade of his life was therefore dedicated to such healing and mending.

During his last years Merton often seemed not to be a good Catholic, especially as that word was defined before Vatican II changed the image of the church. His individualism contradicted the traditional character of the religious vocation and certainly the common ideal of the monastic life. In his writings he questioned the validity of the hierarchical system of both the church and the medieval society in which its roots are so firmly planted. He repudiated the church's attitude toward non-Catholic religions and non-European cultures as in the Jesuit experience in China and the Spanish experience in America. He even questioned the patriarchal form of the Christian family. And he suggested that the church abandon all her temporal rights, riches, and privileges to attain authenticity in poverty.

Yet in a deeper sense Merton was a very good Catholic, for he believed in, preached, and tried to help establish the world unity which has always been his church's central theme. He transcended the Thomistic interpretation of unity, viewing it in a more deeply human sense than most other Catholic theologians until Vatican II, but the theme of unity was still central in his thought. His apparent unorthodoxy lay in his willingness to adopt non-Thomistic methods to achieve the ideal, but he had to be unorthodox because Thomism had left him no program for social reform. A product of the Middle Ages, adopted as the official Roman Catholic theology by the Council of Trent in the sixteenth century, Thomism limited social action to personal acts of charity, a form which Merton approved but found inadequate for modern secular society with its complex problems. When the church broke free of its protective shell in the mid-twentieth century, its voices of reform had no traditional code of social reform, no methodology for reform, and they simply had to create. Merton himself admitted that the church was behind in social thinking, that it had been closed both to the problems and to the solutions being devised for too long, and he taught that the church must listen to the world to understand the problems and to get suggestions for their solution. He used "alien" methods to accomplish the traditional ideal of unity.

Merton's favorite religious book was Dante's *Divine Comedy,* especially the "Paradiso." This book doubtless influenced his thinking, for Dante described heaven in much the same way Merton described the new social order of which he dreamed. Dante's heaven was a place of perfect unity and harmony, a place where every person and activity is in accord with God who is himself referred to as the unifying one. Heaven is the white rose of mystical perfection and spiritual unity with perfect proportions and divine balance. Whereas Dante's guide through the inferno and the purgatorio is Virgil, the symbol of human wisdom, and his guide through most of the paradiso is Beatrice, the symbol of love, his guide in the presence of the Virgin and God is Saint Bernard, the symbol of contemplation. Bernard, the man of living love, who found true harmony and peace in the world through contemplation, leads Dante to God, for the presence of God is a place of contemplation. For Merton, social harmony as well as spiritual harmony will develop in proportion to the amount of contemplation in a society, for only through contemplation can one gain unity with himself, his fellowman, and God.

The value of Merton's social criticism lies not in its originality, for his concept of unity is medieval and his methods for achieving such unity were borrowed from contemporary secular forms of social action. But he did make clear to modern, secular man the almost forgotten thought of medieval monasticism and simultaneously introduced modern secular thought and social methods to his relatively isolated church. He applied the traditional monastic concept of peace as the fruit of charity and contemplation to modern world affairs. He brought the message of the church to modern secular man and the message of modern secular man to the church. By living first in New York City and then in Gethsemani Abbey, Merton lived in two ages, the modern and the medieval, and he was able to bridge a great gap, relating the lessons of antiquity to his own age, using the skills of his own age to implement the wisdom of the ages. For this labor all modern men are in his debt.

In his attitude toward religious dialogue and synthesis, as in his openness to the world and his willingness to help solve its problems, Merton was far ahead of his time. He sometimes overlooked important questions of implementation while looking ahead to a vision of unity that lay in the future. He is a prime candidate for patron saint to a new generation that rejects a world divided into races, nations, and religions, a generation that seeks through action, words, and prayers to build a new world of unity. Because of his life, his love, and not least his poetic vision, he will have a wider audience in the future than he has had in the past. Perhaps the Age of Aquarius will be the age of one of the most outstanding Aquarians, Thomas Merton. Merton was a Catholic, but he was more Christian than Catholic, more religious than Christian, more human than religious.

Bibliography

Books

Thirty Poems. New York: New Directions, 1944.

A Man in the Divided Sea. New York: New Directions, 1946.

Figures for an Apocalypse. New York: New Directions, 1948.

Cistercian Contemplatives. New York: Marbridge Printing Company, Inc., 1948.

The Seven Storey Mountain. New York: Harcourt, Brace and Company, 1948. (New American Library Paperback, 1963.)

What Is Contemplation? Holy Cross, Ind.: St. Mary's College Press, 1948.

Exile Ends in Glory. Milwaukee: The Bruce Publishing Company, 1948.

Seeds of Contemplation. New York: New Directions, 1949. (Dell, 1960.)

The Waters of Siloe. New York: Harcourt, Brace and Company, 1949. (Doubleday Image, 1962.)

The Tears of the Blind Lions. New York: New Directions, 1949.

What Are These Wounds? Milwaukee: The Bruce Publishing Company, 1950.

The Ascent to Truth. New York: Harcourt, Brace and Company, 1951. (Viking Compass, 1959.)

A Balanced Life of Prayer. Trappist, Ky.: Abbey of Gethsemani, 1951.

The Sign of Jonas. New York: Harcourt, Brace and Company, 1953. (Doubleday Image, 1956.)

Bread in the Wilderness. New York: New Directions, 1953.

The Last of the Fathers. New York: Harcourt, Brace and Company, 1954.

No Man Is an Island. New York: Harcourt, Brace and Company, 1955. (Doubleday Image, 1967.)

The Living Bread. New York: Farrar, Straus and Cudahy, 1956.

Silence in Heaven. New York: Studio Publications and Thomas Y. Crowell, 1956.

The Strange Islands. New York: New Directions, 1957.

The Tower of Babel. New York: New Directions, 1957.

The Silent Life. New York: Farrar, Straus, 1957. (Dell, 1959.)

Thoughts in Solitude. New York: Farrar, Straus and Cudahy, 1958.

Monastic Peace. Saint Paul, Minn.: North Central Publishing Company, 1958.

The Secular Journal of Thomas Merton. New York: Farrar, Straus, 1959. (Dell, 1960.)

Selected Poems of Thomas Merton. New York: New Directions, 1959. (Enlarged edition, 1967.)

The Wisdom of the Desert. New York: New Directions, 1960.

Disputed Questions. New York: Farrar, Straus, 1960. (New American Library, 1965.)

The Behavior of Titans. New York: New Directions, 1961.

New Seeds of Contemplation. New York: New Directions, 1961.

The New Man. New York: Farrar, Straus, 1961. (New American Library, 1963.)

A Thomas Merton Reader. Edited by Thomas P. McDonnell. New York: Harcourt, Brace and World, Inc., 1962.

Original Child Bomb. New York: New Directions, 1962.

Breakthrough to Peace. New York: New Directions, 1962.

Life and Holiness. New York: Herder and Herder, 1963. (Doubleday Image, 1964.)

Emblems of a Season of Fury. New York: New Directions, 1963.

Seeds of Destruction. New York: Farrar, Straus and Cudahy, 1964. (Macmillan, 1967.)

The Way of Chuang Tzu. New York: New Directions, 1965.

Gandhi on Non-Violence. New York: New Directions, 1965.

Seasons of Celebration. New York: Farrar, Straus and Giroux, 1965.

Raids on the Unspeakable. New York: New Directions, 1966.

Conjectures of a Guilty Bystander. Garden City, N.Y.: Doubleday and Company, Inc., 1966.

Redeeming the Time. London: Burns and Oates Limited, 1966.

Mystics and Zen Masters. New York: Straus and Giroux, 1967. (Delta, 1969.)

Cables to the Ace. New York: New Directions, 1968.

Faith and Violence. South Bend, Ind.: University of Notre Dame Press, 1968.

Zen and the Birds of Appetite. New York: New Directions, 1968.

The Plague. Religious Dimensions in Literature. The Seabury Reading Program. RDL7. Lee A. Belford, general editor. New York: The Seabury Press, 1968.

Contemplative Prayer. New York: Herder and Herder, 1969.

The Geography of Lograire. New York: New Directions, 1969.

My Argument with the Gestapo. Garden City, N.Y.: Doubleday and Company, Inc., 1969.

Articles

"Absurdity in Sacred Decoration." *Worship* 34 (April 1960):248–55.

"Active and Contemplative Orders." *Commonweal* 46 (December 5, 1947):192–96.

"And the Children of Birmingham." *Saturday Review* 46 (August 10, 1963):32.

"Art and Worship." *Sponsa Regis* 31 (December 1959):114–17.

"The Black Revolution." *Ramparts* 2 (Christmas 1963):4–23.

"Boris Pasternak." *Jubilee* 7 (July 1959):17–31.

"Buddhism and the Modern World." *Cross Currents* 16 (Fall 1966):495–99.

"Called Out of Darkness." *Sponsa Regis* 33 (November 1961): 61–71.

"Can We Survive Nihilism?" *Saturday Review* 50 (April 15, 1967):16–19.

"The Catholic and Creativity." *American Benedictine Review* 11 (September-December 1960):197–213.

"The Challenge of Responsibility." *Saturday Review* 48 (February 13, 1965):28–30.

"Christian Action in World Crisis." *Blackfriars* 43 (June 1962): 256–68.

"Christian Culture Needs Oriental Wisdom." *Catholic World* 195 (May 1962):72–79.

"Christian Ethics and Nuclear War." *Catholic Worker* 28 (March 1962):2, 7.

"Christian Freedom and Monastic Formation." *American Benedictine Review* 13 (September 1962):289–313.

"Christian Morality and Nuclear War." *Way* 19 (June 1963):12–22.

"Christianity and Mass Movements." *Cross Currents* 9 (Summer 1959):201–11.

"Classic Chinese Thought." *Jubilee* 8 (January 1961):26–32.

"A Conference on Prayer." *Sisters Today* 41 (April 1970):455.

"Conjectures of a Guilty Bystander." *Life* 61 (August 5, 1966):
60–73.

"Contemplation in a World of Action." *Bloomin' Newman* 2
(April 1968):1–5.

"The Contemplative and the Atheist." *Schema XIII* 1 (January
1970):11–18.

"The Council and Monasticism." In *The Impact of Vatican II,*
edited by Jude P. Dougherty. St. Louis, Mo.: B. Herder Book
Company, 1966.

"Creative Silence." *Baptist Student* 48 (February 1969):18–22.

"Elegy for a Trappist." *Commonweal* 75 (December 9, 1966):294.

"An Elegy for Ernest Hemingway." *Commonweal* 74 (September
22, 1961):513.

"Elegy for James Thurber." *Commonweal* 76 (July 13, 1962):396.

"Ethics and War, A Footnote." *Catholic Worker* 28 (April 1962):2.

"Few Questions and Fewer Answers." *Harper's Magazine* 231
(November 1965):79–81.

"First Lesson about Man." *Saturday Review* 52 (January 11,
1969):21.

"Flannery O'Connor." *Jubilee* 12 (November 1964):49.

"For My Brother." *Catholic Art Quarterly* 8 (Easter 1945):29.

"Gandhi and the One-Eyed Giant." *Jubilee* 12 (January 1965):12–17.

"The Gentle Revolutionary." *Ramparts* 3 (December 1964):28–32.

"Godless Christianity?" *Katallagete* (Winter 1967–1968):15–21.

"The Guns of Fort Knox." *Sign* 37 (August 1957):39.

"The Honest to God Debate." *Commonweal* 80 (August 21,
1964):573–74.

"The Hot Summer of Sixty-Seven." *Katallagete* (Winter 1967–
1968): 28–34.

"How It Is—Apologies to an Unbeliever." *Harper's Magazine* 233
(November 1966):36–39.

"I Have Chosen You." *Sponsa Regis* 30 (September 1958):1–6.

"'In the Ruins of New York." *Commonweal* 46 (June 6, 1947):182.

"Is Mysticism Normal?" *Commonweal* 51 (November 4, 1949):
94–98.

"Is the World a Problem?" *Commonweal* 84 (June 3, 1966):305–9.

"Learning to Live." In *University of the Heights,* edited by Wesley
First. Garden City, N.Y.: Doubleday and Company, Inc., 1969.

"Let the Poor Man Speak." *Jubilee* 8 (October 1960):18–21.

"Letter to America." *Commonweal* 45 (February 7, 1947):419.

"Love and Maturity." *Sponsa Regis* 32 (October 1960):44–53.
"Man Is a Gorilla with a Gun." *New Blackfriars* 46 (May 1965): 452–57.
"Manifestation of Conscience and Spiritual Direction." *Sponsa Regis* 30 (July 1959):277–82.
"Message to Poets from Thomas Merton." *Americas* 16 (April 1964):29.
"Monks and Hunters." *Commonweal* 54 (April 20, 1951):39–40.
"The Monk and Sacred Art." *Sponsa Regis* 28 (May 1957):231–34.
"Monk in the Diaspora." *Commonweal* 79 (March 20, 1964): 741–45.
"The Negro Revolt." *Jubilee* 10 (September 1963):39–43.
"Nhat Hanh Is My Brother." *Jubilee* 14 (August 1966):11.
"Nuclear War and Christian Responsibility." *Commonweal* 75 (February 9, 1962):509–13.
"On the Anniversary of My Baptism." *Commonweal* 43 (April 12, 1946):640.
"An Open Letter to the American Hierarchy: Schema XIII and the Modern World." *Worldview* 8 (September 1965):4–7.
"The Other Side of Despair." *Critic* 24 (October–November 1965):12–23.
"The Ox Mountain Parable of Meng Tzu." *Commonweal* 74 (May 12, 1961):174.
"The Pasternak Affair in Perspective." *Thought* 34 (Winter 1959): 485–517.
"Peace and Revolution: A Footnote from Ulysses." *Peace* 3 (Fall–Winter 1968–1969):5–10.
"Poetry and Contemplation: A Reappraisal." *Commonweal* 69 (October 24, 1958):87–92.
"Poetry and the Contemplative Life." *Commonweal* 46 (July 4, 1947):280–86.
"Poverty." *Catholic Worker* 15 (April 1949):3.
"Prayer for Guidance in Art." *Liturgical Arts* 27 (May 1959):64.
"The Psalms as Poetry." *Commonweal* 59 (October 30, 1953):79–81.
"Rain and the Rhinoceros." *Holiday* 37 (May 1965):8–16.
"Raissa Maritain's Poems." *Jubilee* 10 (April 1963):27.
"The Reader." *Atlantic Monthly* 184 (December 1949):55.
"Reality, Art, and Prayer." *Commonweal* 61 (March 25, 1955): 658–59.
"Religion and the Bomb." *Jubilee* 10 (May 1962):7–13.

"Renewal in Monastic Education." *Cistercian Studies* 3 (Third Quarter 1968):247–52.

"The Root of War." *Catholic Worker* 28 (October 1961):1, 7–8.

"The Sacred City." *Catholic Worker* 34 (January 1968):4–6.

"Self Denial and the Christian." *Commonweal* 51 (March 31, 1950):649–53.

"The Shakers." *Jubilee* 11 (February 1964):36–41.

"The Shelter Ethic." *Catholic Worker* 28 (November 1961):1, 5.

"The Shoshoneans." *Catholic Worker* 33 (June 1967):5–6.

"Spirituality for the Age of Overkill." *Continuum* 1 (Spring 1963):9–21.

"Temperament and Meditation." *Sponsa Regis* 31 (June 1960): 296–99.

"Terror and the Absurd: Violence and Non-Violence in Albert Camus." *Motive* 29 (February 1969):5–15.

"Thomas Merton on the Strike." *Catholic Worker* 28 (February 1962):7.

"Three Letters." *Motive* 25 (November 1964):4–8.

"We Have To Make Ourselves Heard." *Catholic Worker* 28 (May 1962):4–6.

"We Have To Make Ourselves Heard—Continued." *Catholic Worker* 28 (June 1962):4–5.

"What Is Meditation?" *Sponsa Regis* 31 (February 1960):180–87.

"Why Some Men Look Up to Planets and Heroes." *America* 108 (March 30, 1963):433.

"Zen: Sense and Sensibility." *America* 108 (May 25, 1963):752–54.

Manuscripts

(The following manuscripts were sent to James T. Baker by either Thomas Merton himself or by his librarian Brother Benedict after Merton's death. Some of them have subsequently been published, some have not, some will doubtless be published under this title or a new one in the future. I have used these manuscripts extensively, but I have not quoted directly from them, for to have done so would have violated the rules of the Thomas Merton Legacy Trust.)

"Auschwitz: A Family Camp." (Later published in *Peace News*, August 1967.)

"Camus and the Catholic Church."

"A Christian Looks at Zen."

"Christianity and Defense in the Nuclear Age."

"The Church and the 'Godless World.'"

"Civil Disobedience and Non-Violent Revolution." (Merton submitted this manuscript as a report requested by the National Commission on the Causes and Prevention of Violence.)

"The Contemplative and the Atheist."

"D. T. Suzuki, the Man and His Work."

"Ecumenism and Monastic Renewal."

"Edifying Cables."

"Love and Need." (This manuscript was published as "A Buyer's Market for Love?" *Ave Maria* 104 [December 24, 1966].)

"Marxist Theory and Monastic Theoria." (This manuscript was taken from the tape of Merton's last public speech, delivered in Bangkok, December 10, 1968.)

"Monastic Experience and East-West Dialogue." (This manuscript is now pp. 72–82 of *The World Religions Speak,* edited by Finley P. Dunne, Jr., and published in The Hague.

"A New Christian Consciousness?"

"Notes on the Future of Monasticism." (This manuscript will be included in Doubleday's *Contemplation in a World of Action.*)

"Openness and Cloister."

"Passivity and Abuse of Authority."

"Religion and Race in the United States." (This manuscript has been published in *New Blackfriars* 46 [January 1965]:218–25.)

"A Ruler's Examination of Conscience."

"Symbolism—Communication or Communion?"

"War and the Crisis of Language."

Notes

Chapter One

[1] Thomas Merton, *The Seven Storey Mountain* (New York, 1963), p. 10.

[2] See ibid., pp. 11–27, which contains his musings about his early religious life and his mother.

[3] See ibid., pp. 26–32, which describes his experience at Douglaston.

[4] See ibid., pp. 35–65, for a discussion of his experiences in France.

[5] Ibid., p 69.

[6] Ibid., p. 77.

[7] See ibid., pp. 109–17, for a discussion of his experiences in Rome.

[8] See ibid., pp. 118–21, where he talks about his search for religion in America.

[9] See ibid., pp. 133–37 for an account of his brush with communism.

[10] Thomas Merton, "Learning to Live," *University of the Heights,* ed. Wesley First (Garden City, N.Y., 1969), pp. 197–98.

[11] Will Lissner, "Toast to the Avant-Garde," *Catholic World* 166 (February 1948):427.

[12] Merton, *The Seven Storey Mountain,* p. 186.

[13] Ibid., p. 142.

[14] See ibid., pp. 188–96, where he discusses his thesis.

[15] Thomas Merton, *My Argument with the Gestapo* (Garden City, N.Y., 1969), p. 259.

[16] Lissner, "Toast to the Avant-Garde," p. 427.

[17] See Merton, *The Seven Storey Mountain,* pp. 259–92, where he discusses his experiences with the Franciscans.

[18] See ibid., pp. 302–9, for his discussion of the war.

[19] Thomas Merton, *The Secular Journal of Thomas Merton* (New York, 1960), p. 155.

[20] Merton, *The Seven Storey Mountain,* p. 318.

[21] Ibid., p. 351.

[22] Merton, *The Secular Journal of Thomas Merton,* p. 223.

[23] Paul Elmen, "Already in Custody," *Christian Century* 76 (October 21, 1959):1215.

[24] Merton, *The Seven Storey Mountain,* p. 377.

[25] Ibid., p. 400–401.

[26] Thomas Merton, *The Sign of Jonas* (New York, 1953), pp. 10–11.

[27] Ibid., p. 40.

[28] Ibid., pp. 78–79.

[29] Thomas Merton, "A Conference on Prayer," *Sisters Today* 41 (April 1970):455.

[30] Thomas P. McDonnell, "An Interview with Thomas Merton," *Motive* 28 (October 1967):32.

[31] Merton, *The Sign of Jonas,* p. 125.

[32] For a revealing summary of Merton's daily life as a hermit, see "Meditation in the Woods," published in the Summer 1967 edition of *Hudson Review* and condensed for the January 1968 edition of *Catholic Digest.*

[33] See Edward Rice, "Thomas Merton Today," *Jubilee* 13 (March 1966):32.

[34] *Time,* December 20, 1968, p. 65.

[35] Thomas Merton, "Marxist Theory and Monastic Theoria," p. 9. (This

speech will soon be published as part of Merton's papers written on the trip to Asia by Notre Dame Press and will appear as part of the appendix in New Directions' *Asian Journal of Thomas Merton*. I used a personal copy, taken from the original tape and sent to me by Brother Benedict of Gethsemani, March 1969.)

[36] Merton, *The Seven Storey Mountain*, p. 412.

[37] Thomas Merton, *Cables to the Ace* (New York, 1968), p. 24.

[38] John Moffitt, "Bangkok: New Charter for Monasticism," *America* 120 (January 18, 1969):64.

Chapter Two

[1] Thomas Merton, *The Seven Storey Mountain* (New York, 1963), p. 314.

[2] Thomas Merton, "Active and Contemplative Orders," *Commonweal* 47 (December 5, 1947):195.

[3] Thomas Merton, *The Waters of Siloe* (Garden City, N.Y., 1962), p. 17.

[4] Ibid., p. 30.

[5] Y. H. Krikorian, "Fruits of Mysticism," *New Republic* 121 (September 12, 1949):17.

[6] Thomas Merton, *The Ascent to Truth* (New York, 1959), p. 5.

[7] Thomas Merton, *The Sign of Jonas* (New York, 1953), p. 322.

[8] Thomas Merton, "Is the World a Problem?" *Commonweal* 84 (June 3, 1966):305.

[9] Ibid.

[10] Thomas P. McDonnell, "An Interview with Thomas Merton," *Motive* 28 (October 1967):32–33.

[11] Thomas Merton, "Monks and Hunters," *Commonweal* 54 (April 20, 1951):39–40.

[12] This information was gained through a private interview with Merton at Gethsemani Abbey on February 28, 1968.

[13] Merton, *The Sign of Jonas*, pp. 91–92.

[14] Thomas Merton, *Conjectures of a Guilty Bystander* (Garden City, N.Y., 1966), pp. 140–41.

[15] Merton, *The Sign of Jonas*, p. 323.

[16] Thomas Merton, *Raids on the Unspeakable* (New York, 1966), pp. 54–56.

[17] Ibid., p. 62.

[18] Merton, *Conjectures of a Guilty Bystander*, p. 45.

[19] Ibid., p. 25.

[20] Thomas Merton, "A Ruler's Examination of Conscience," p. 1. (I used a personal copy of this introduction to Fenelon's works, sent me by the author in 1967.)

[21] Thomas Merton, "The Challenge of Responsibility," *Saturday Review* 48 (February 13, 1965):28–30.

[22] Thomas Merton, *Life and Holiness* (Garden City, N.Y., 1964), p. 24.

[23] Thomas Merton, "Called Out of Darkness," *Sponsa Regis* 33 (November 1961):66.

[24] Merton, *Life and Holiness*, p. 93.

[25] Coleman McCarthy "The Old Order Changeth . . . Trappists Open Up to World," *Louisville Times,* January 9, 1969.

[26] Merton, *The Sign of Jonas*, p. 322.

Chapter Three

[1] For a critique of this part of Merton's thought, see Aelred Graham's "Thomas Merton, A Modern Man in Reverse," *Atlantic Monthly* 191 (January 1953):74.

[2] Thomas Merton, *Life and Holiness* (Garden City, N.Y, 1964), p. 13.

[3] For a critique of this area of Merton's thought, see John Logan's "Babel Theory," *Commonweal* 66 (July 4, 1957):357.

[4] Thomas Merton, *Seeds of Contemplation* (New York, 1960), pp. 52–54.

[5] Thomas Merton, *The New Man* (New York, 1963), pp. 12–15.

[6] Merton, *Seeds of Contemplation*, p. 16.

[7] Thomas Merton, *Raids on the Unspeakable* (New York, 1966), p. 17.

[8] Thomas Merton, *Mystics and Zen Masters* (New York, 1967), p. 204.

[9] Thomas Merton, *Disputed Questions* (New York, 1965), p. x.

[10] Merton, *Raids on the Unspeakable*, p. 22.

[11] Thomas Merton, "Renewal in Monastic Education," *Cistercian Studies* 3 (Third Quarter 1968):247–52.

[12] Merton, *Life and Holiness*, p. 28.

[13] Thomas Merton, "Contemplation in a World of Action," *Bloomin' Newman* 2 (April 1968):5.

[14] Merton, *Life and Holiness*, p. 89.

[15] Merton, *Raids on the Unspeakable*, p. 22.

[16] Thomas Merton, *Conjectures of a Guilty Bystander* (Garden City, N.Y., 1966), p. 141.

[17] Ibid.

[18] Merton, *Seeds of Contemplation*, pp. 35–36.

[19] Ibid., p. 42.

[20] Ibid., p. 43.

[21] Ibid., p. 80.

[22] Thomas Merton, *New Seeds of Contemplation* (New York, 1961), pp. 52–80.

[23] Thomas Merton, "Notes on the Future of Monasticism," p. 1. (This manuscript will be published in *Contemplation in a World of Action* to be released by Doubleday in 1971.)

[24] Thomas Merton, *The Silent Life* (New York, 1959), pp. 19–22.

[25] Ibid., pp. 152–54.

[26] Merton, *Seeds of Contemplation*, p. 50.

[27] Merton, *Life and Holiness*, p. 93.

[28] Ibid., pp. 100–101.

[29] Thomas Merton, "Is the World a Problem?" *Commonweal* 84 (June 3, 1966):305.

[30] Merton, *Seeds of Contemplation*, p. 50.

[31] Merton, *Conjectures of a Guilty Bystander*, p. 36.

[32] Thomas Merton, *Faith and Violence* (South Bend, Ind., 1968), p. 256.

[33] Thomas Merton, "Conjectures of a Guilty Bystander," *Life* 61 (August 5, 1966):62.

[34] Thomas Merton, "Rain and the Rhinoceros," *Holiday* 37 (May 1965):8.

[35] Ibid.

[36] Thomas Merton, "First Lesson about Man," *Saturday Review* 52 (January 11, 1969):21.

[37] Merton, *Faith and Violence*, pp. 247–48.

[38] Merton, *Conjectures of a Guilty Bystander*, p. 23.

[39] Thomas Merton, *Figures for an Apocalypse* (New York, 1947), pp. 22–24.

[40] Thomas Merton, *The Strange Islands* (New York, 1957), p. 51.

[41] Ibid., pp. 65–66.

[42] Ibid., p. 66.

[43] Ibid., pp. 71–72.

[44] Ibid., p. 72.

[45] Merton, *Disputed Questions*, p. 145.

[46] Merton, *New Seeds of Contemplation*, p. 55.

[47] Thomas Merton, *The Ascent to Truth* (New York, 1959), p. 4.

[48] Merton, "Conjectures of a Guilty Bystander," p. 62.

[49] Merton, *Raids on the Unspeakable*, p. 69.

[50] Merton, "Rain and the Rhinoceros," p. 16. (On pages 65–71 of Merton's book *The Behavior of Titans* the reader will find "A Signed Confession of Crimes against the State," a letter in which Merton admits spending an idle hour in the woods, watching the animals and insects and listening to the song of the birds.)

[51] Merton, *Disputed Questions*, p. 145.

[52] Thomas Merton, *Seeds of Destruction* (New York, 1965), pp. 139–40.

[53] Ibid., p. 220.

[54] Thomas Merton, "Monk in the Diaspora," *Commonweal* 89 (March 20, 1964):741.

[55] Merton, *Seeds of Destruction*, pp. 133–35.

[56] Merton, "Monk in the Diaspora," pp. 738–45.

[57] Merton, *Seeds of Destruction*, p. 153.

[58] Ibid., p. 155.

[59] Merton, "Monk in the Diaspora," p. 744.

[60] Merton, *Seeds of Destruction*, p. 218.

[61] Merton, "Notes on the Future of Monasticism," p. 3.

[62] Merton, "Renewal in Monastic Education," p. 251.

Chapter Four

[1] Thomas P. McDonnell, "An Interview with Thomas Merton," *Motive* 28 (October 1967):33–34.

[2] Thomas Merton, *Disputed Questions* (New York, 1965), p. 51.

[3] Thomas Merton, *Monastic Peace* (Saint Paul, Minn., 1958), p. 46.

[4] Ibid., p. 44.

[5] Thomas Merton, *Emblems of a Season of Fury* (New York, 1963), p. 89.

[6] Merton, *Disputed Questions*, p. 51.

[7] Ibid., p. 60.

[8] Thomas Merton, *Figures for an Apocalypse* (New York, 1948), pp. 20–21.

[9] Thomas Merton, "Is the World a Problem?" *Commonweal* 84 (June 3, 1966):309.

[10] Thomas Merton, *A Thomas Merton Reader*, ed. Thomas P. McDonnell (New York, 1962), p. 151.

[11] Thomas Merton, *Conjectures of a Guilty Bystander* (Garden City, N.Y., 1966), p. 33.

[12] Merton, *Disputed Questions*, p. 103.

[13] Thomas Merton, "Christianity and Mass Movements," *Cross Currents* 9 (Summer 1959):203–4.

[14] Merton, *Disputed Questions*, p. 116.

[15] Ibid., p. 114.

[16] Merton, "Christianity and Mass Movements," p. 209.

[17] Ibid., pp. 205–6.

[18] Merton, *Conjectures of a Guilty Bystander*, pp. 23–28.

[19] Merton, *Emblems of a Season of Fury*, pp. 70–89.

[20] Thomas Merton, "Terror and the Absurd: Violence and Non-Violence in Albert Camus," *Motive* 29 (February 1969):5.

[21] Merton, *Emblems of a Season of Fury*, p. 73.

[22] Ibid., p. 86.

[23] Thomas Merton, "Let the Poor Man Speak," *Jubilee* 8 (October 1960):18.

[24] Ibid., p. 19.

[25] Ibid., p. 21.

[26] Thomas Merton, "The Root of War," *Catholic Worker* 28 (October 1961):1.

[27] Thomas Merton, "Nuclear War and Christian Responsibility," *Commonweal* 75 (February 19, 1962):509–11.

[28] Thomas Merton, "We Have To Make Ourselves Heard," *Catholic Worker* 28 (May 1962):4.

[29] Thomas Merton, "Christian Morality and Nuclear War," *Way* 19 (June 1963):13.

[30] Thomas Merton, *Breakthrough to Peace* (New York, 1962), pp. 9–10.

[31] Merton, "We Have To Make Ourselves Heard," p. 4.

[32] Thomas Merton, "The Shelter Ethic," *Catholic Worker* 28 (November 1961):5.

[33] Merton, "We Have To Make Ourselves Heard," p. 4.

[34] Thomas Merton, "Christian Ethics and Nuclear War," *Catholic Worker* 28 (March 1962):2.

[35] Thomas Merton, "Ethics and War, A Footnote," *Catholic Worker* 28 (April 1962):2.

[36] Merton, *Breakthrough to Peace*, pp. 89–90.

[37] Merton, "We Have To Make Ourselves Heard," p. 4.

[38] Merton, "The Root of War," pp. 7–8.

[39] Thomas Merton, "We Have To Make Ourselves Heard—Continued," *Catholic Worker* 28 (June 1962):4.

[40] Merton, *A Thomas Merton Reader*, p. 293.

[41] Merton, "Christian Morality and Nuclear War," p. 13.

[42] Merton, "We Have To Make Ourselves Heard," p. 4.

[43] Thomas Merton, "Passivity and the Abuse of Authority," pp. 1–2. (This manuscript was sent to me by the author in 1967.)

[44] Thomas Merton, "An Open Letter to the American Hierarchy: Schema XIII and the Modern World," *Worldview* 8 (September 1965):7.

[45] Merton, *Conjectures of a Guilty Bystander*, p. 271.

[46] Merton, *Breakthrough to Peace*, p. 108.

[47] Merton, "Nuclear War and Christian Responsibility," p. 512.

[48] Merton, *A Thomas Merton Reader*, pp. 294–95.

[49] Merton, "Ethics and War, A Footnote," p. 2.

[50] Merton, "Christian Ethics and Nuclear War," p. 7.

[51] Merton, "We Have To Make Ourselves Heard—Continued," p. 4.

[52] McDonnell, "An Interview with Thomas Merton," p. 38.

[53] Thomas Merton, "Christianity and Defense in the Nuclear Age," pp. 1–2. (This manuscript was sent to me by the author in 1967.)

[54] Merton, *Breakthrough to Peace*, p. 94.

[55] Merton, "Christianity and Defense in the Nuclear Age," pp. 3–4.

[56] Merton, "Christian Morality and Nuclear War," p. 22.

[57] Merton, "We Have To Make Ourselves Heard," p. 4.

[58] Ibid., p. 5.

[59] Merton, "Christian Morality and Nuclear War," p. 20.

[60] Merton, "The Root of War," p. 7.

[61] Merton, *A Thomas Merton Reader*, p. 288.

[62] Merton, "The Shelter Ethic," p. 1.

[63] Merton, "The Root of War," p. 1.

[64] Merton, *A Thomas Merton Reader*, p. 294.

[65] Merton, "We Have To Make Ourselves Heard—Continued," p. 5.

[66] Merton, *A Thomas Merton Reader*, pp. 301–2.

[67] Ibid., pp. 17–20, 302.

[68] Merton, "The Root of War," p. 8.

[69] Merton, "Christian Morality and Nuclear War," p. 16.

[70] Merton, "Nuclear War and Christian Responsibility," p. 509.

[71] Merton, *A Thomas Merton Reader*, p. 297.

[72] Merton, "We Have To Make Ourselves Heard," pp. 4–5.

[73] Merton, "Christian Ethics and Nuclear War," p. 7.

[74] Merton, *Breakthrough to Peace*, pp. 10–11.

[75] Merton, "We Have To Make Ourselves Heard—Continued," p. 5.

[76] McDonnell, "An Interview with Thomas Merton," p. 38.
[77] Merton, "The Root of War," p. 8.
[78] Merton, *A Thomas Merton Reader*, p. 301.
[79] Merton, "We Have To Make Ourselves Heard—Continued," p. 4.
[80] Merton, "We Have To Make Ourselves Heard," p. 5.
[81] Merton, "Nuclear War and Christian Responsibility," p. 511.
[82] Merton, *A Thomas Merton Reader*, p. 296.
[83] Merton, "We Have To Make Ourselves Heard," p. 4.
[84] Thomas Merton, *Raids on the Unspeakable* (New York, 1966), p. 48.
[85] Ibid., pp. 45–49.
[86] Thomas Merton, *Seeds of Destruction* (New York, 1964), p. 204.
[87] Thomas Merton, *Original Child Bomb* (New York, 1962), pp. 1–15.
[88] Thomas Merton, "Thomas Merton on the Strike," *Catholic Worker* 28 (February 1962):7.
[89] Merton, "Nuclear War and Christian Responsibility," p. 511.
[90] Merton, "Christian Ethics and Nuclear War," p. 7. (This article evoked bitter responses from Catholics working in nuclear defense plants. See *Commonweal*, April 20, 1962.)
[91] Merton, "We Have To Make Ourselves Heard—Continued," p. 4.
[92] Merton, *Seeds of Destruction*, pp. 125–26.
[93] Ibid., p. 186.
[94] Merton, *A Thomas Merton Reader*, p. 301.
[95] Thomas Merton, *The Ascent to Truth* (New York, 1959), p. 7.
[96] Merton, *Disputed Questions*, p. 150.
[97] Merton, *Raids on the Unspeakable*, pp. 4–5.

Chapter Five

[1] Thomas Merton, *Faith and Violence* (South Bend, Ind., 1968), p. 6.
[2] Thomas Merton, "Civil Disobedience and Non-Violent Revolution," p. 1 (manuscript).
[3] Thomas Merton, *A Man in the Divided Sea* (New York, 1946), p. 42.
[4] Thomas Merton, "The Shoshoneans," *Catholic Worker* 33 (June 1967):5.
[5] Merton, *Faith and Violence*, p. 3.
[6] Thomas Merton, "Conjectures of a Guilty Bystander," *Life* 61 (August 5, 1966):71–72.
[7] Thomas Merton, *Seeds of Destruction* (New York, 1965), pp. 41–42.
[8] Thomas Merton, "The Hot Summer of Sixty-Seven," *Katallagete* (Winter 1967–1968):34.
[9] Merton, *Seeds of Destruction*, pp. 43–44.
[10] Ibid., pp. 22–28.
[11] Ibid., pp. 212–14
[12] Ibid., pp. 47–51.
[13] Ibid., p. 209.
[14] Ibid., p. 38.
[15] Ibid., p. 62.
[16] Ibid., p. 39.
[17] Ibid., p. 66.
[18] Ibid., pp. 39–40.
[19] Ibid., p. 69.
[20] Ibid., p. 56.
[21] Thomas Merton, "The Black Revolution," *Ramparts* 2 (Christmas 1963):23.
[22] Merton, *Seeds of Destruction*, p. 14.
[23] Ibid., p. 46.
[24] Thomas Merton, "Religion and Race in the United States," p. 1. (This

manuscript was published as an article in *New Blackjriars,* January 1965, but I used a typewritten copy sent me by the author.)

[25] Merton, "The Hot Summer of Sixty-Seven," p. 28.

[26] Merton, *Seeds of Destruction,* p. 211.

[27] Ibid., p. 16.

[28] Ibid., p. 31.

[29] Ibid., p. 25.

[30] Ibid., pp. 33–38.

[31] Martin Marty's open letter appeared in the August 30, 1967, issue of *National Catholic Reporter,* and Merton's response appeared in the September 6, 1967, issue.

[32] Thomas Merton, *Conjectures of a Guilty Bystander* (Garden City, N.Y., 1966), p. 62.

[33] Thomas Merton, "Auschwitz: A Family Camp," pp. 11–12. (This is from a manuscript sent to me by the author in 1968. It was published in *Peace News,* August 1967.)

[34] Merton, "The Hot Summer of Sixty-Seven," p. 33.

[35] Merton, *Faith and Violence,* p. 129.

[36] Ibid., p. 124.

[37] Merton, "The Hot Summer of Sixty-Seven," p. 28.

[38] Thomas P. McDonnell, "An Interview with Thomas Merton," *Motive* 28 (October 1967):38.

[39] Merton, *Faith and Violence,* p. 41.

[40] Ibid., p. 105.

[41] Ibid., p. 30.

[42] See Part 1 of *Faith and Violence.*

[43] Thomas Merton, *Gandhi on Non-Violence* (New York, 1965), p. 1.

[44] Thomas Merton, "Gandhi and the One-Eyed Giant," *Jubilee* 12 (January 1965):17.

[45] Merton, *Seeds of Destruction,* p. 161.

[46] Merton, *Gandhi on Non-Violence,* p. 20.

[47] Merton, "Gandhi and the One-Eyed Giant," p. 15.

[48] Merton, *Seeds of Destruction,* p. 160.

[49] Merton, "Gandhi and the One-Eyed Giant," p. 16.

[50] Thomas Merton, "The Shelter Ethic," *Catholic Worker* 28 (November 1961):5.

[51] Thomas Merton, "Peace and Revolution: A Footnote from Ulysses," *Peace* 3 (Fall–Winter 1968–1969):10.

[52] Merton, *Gandhi on Non-Violence,* p. 13.

[53] Merton, *Conjectures of a Guilty Bystander,* p. 73.

[54] Merton, "Gandhi and the One-Eyed Giant," pp. 15–16.

[55] Merton, *Gandhi on Non-Violence,* p. 6.

[56] For the best description of the nonviolent approach to civil rights reform, see Martin Luther King, Jr.'s "Letter from a Birmingham Jail," *Liberation,* June 1963.

[57] Merton, *Seeds of Destruction,* p. 96.

[58] Merton, *Conjectures of a Guilty Bystander,* pp. 54–55.

Chapter Six

[1] Thomas Merton, *Seeds of Destruction* (New York, 1965), p. 200.

[2] Ibid.

[3] Thomas Merton, *Mystics and Zen Masters* (New York, 1967), p. 187.

[4] Ibid., p. 165.

[5] Thomas Merton, *Emblems of a Season of Fury* (New York, 1963).

[6] Merton, *Mystics and Zen Masters,* p. 91.

[7] Merton, *Seeds of Destruction*, pp. 190, 207-8.

[8] Thomas Merton, "How It Is—Apologies to an Unbeliever," *Harper's Magazine* 233 (November 1966):36-39.

[9] Merton, *Mystics and Zen Masters*, pp. 255-79.

[10] Merton, *Seeds of Destruction*, pp. 188-89.

[11] Thomas Merton, *Faith and Violence* (South Bend, Ind., 1968), pp. 225-38.

[12] Ibid., p. 238.

[13] Ibid., p. 247.

[14] Ibid., p. 262.

[15] Thomas Merton, *Conjectures of a Guilty Bystander* (Garden City, N.Y., 1966), p. 286.

[16] Thomas Merton, "Christian Culture Needs Oriental Wisdom," *Catholic World* 195 (May 1962):78-79.

[17] Merton, *Mystics and Zen Masters*, pp. 82-90.

[18] Ibid., p. 209.

[19] Thomas Merton, "Nhat Hanh Is My Brother," *Jubilee* 14 (August 1966):11.

[20] Thomas Merton, *The Way of Chuang Tzu* (New York, 1965).

[21] Ibid., p. 11.

[22] Merton, *Mystics and Zen Masters*, pp. 57-58.

[23] Thomas Merton, "The Ox Mountain Parable of Meng Tzu," *Commonweal* 74 (May 12, 1961):174.

[24] Merton, *Mystics and Zen Masters*, pp. 225-28.

[25] Ibid., pp. 248-49.

[26] Ibid., pp. 13-14.

[27] Ibid., p. 254.

[28] Ibid., pp. 65-69.

Index

"Active and Contemplative Order," 29
Ad Petri Cathedram, 91
Aeschylus, 104
Africa, 75
African Genesis, 115
America (U.S.): post-World War II mood in, 22; Merton feels responsible for, 38; criticizes politics of, 42, 121; affluence of, 56, 133; The American Community, 61, 64; people of, 65; Americanism, 72–73, 113; as the Earthly Paradise, 72–73; mass media of, 80; mentality of, 80; Catholic hierarchy in, 82; action of, in Viet Nam, 92; attitude of, 97; structure of life in, 98; violence in, 98–99, 114; racial attitudes of, 99; future of, 100; prestige of, threatened in Viet Nam, 101, 113; how to save, 105; Negro alienated from society of, 107; Totalitarian party in, 108; ravaged, 111; of L.B.J., 111; more nonviolent resistance needed in, 116; Merton's absence from life in, 122; did not despair of, 122; Catholic ghettos in, 126
American Community, 61
American Hitler, 110
Americanism, 72–73, 113
American Totalitarian party, 108
America the Earthly Paradise, 72–73
Amos (Old Testament prophet), 113
ancestors, honor of, 136
Anglicanism. *See* Church of England
anti-modern, 66
Apocalypse, 33
Aquarius, age of, 148
Aquinas, Thomas, 8, 127, 132, 140
Arabia, 75, 105
Ardrey, Robert, 115
Aristotle, 140
Arts and Scholasticism, 10
asceticism: need for, 31; practices of, 63

aseity, 10
Asia, Catholic witness in, 25, 77
Asian journal, 138
atheism, 68
atheists, 47
Athens, 137
atomic bomb, 21, 81, 95
Augustine, Saint: on war, 81; interpreter of Plotinus, 127, 140; mentioned, 10, 55, 57–58
Augustinianism, 45
Auschwitz, 110
Australia, 75
average man, 46
Averroes, 140

Babylon, 54, 57
"balance of terror," 78
Baldwin, James, 103
ballistic missiles, 90
Bangkok, Thailand, 26, 135
Bangkok conference, 26
Baptist, black, 123
barbarism, 97
Bardstown, Ky., 13
battles of society, 52
"beatnik," 90
Beatrice, symbol of love, 147
Benedict, Saint, 127
Berchman, Mother, 42
Berenger, 60
Bermuda, 2
Bernard, Saint: symbol of contemplation, 147
Berrigans, Daniel and Philip, 85
Bible, The: discussion of 1 Corinthians 13: 4; read in Rome, 5; Genesis 11: 1–9, 57; Revelation 18: 21–24, 57; Lucan Christmas story, 60
bishops, 83
black and white, civil relationship between, 99–111
Black Power, 107, 110
Black Supremist, 104
Blake, William: influences on Merton, 4, 8; Merton's thesis on, 10–11
Bloom, Leopold: nonviolence of, 120

Body of Christ, 49
Bonhoeffer, Dietrich, 131–33
bourgeois: taste, 6; paternalism, 67
Bramachari, influence on Merton,
　9–10, 135
Bride of Christ, 62
Britain: aristocracy, 4; diplomatic
　service, 6; colonials, 100; rule in
　India, 117; opposed by Ghandi,
　122
Broadway, 57
Bronx, 57
Brothers, African, Asian, European,
　103
Buddha, 142
Buddhists, 47
Bultmann, Rudolf, 131
Byzantine mosaics, 5

Cables to the Ace, 26
Caliban, Tucker, 103–4
Calvin, John, 142
Cambridge University: Merton ac-
　cepted into, 4; unhappy departure
　from, 6
Camus, Albert, 21, 73, 130
Carolingian world view, 70
Carthusians, 18
Catholic Church. *See* Roman Cath-
　olic Church
Catholic Literary Award for 1949,
　Seven Storey Mountain wins, 23
Catholic mass, Merton finds fellow-
　man in, 32
Catholic Press Association Award,
　Figures for an Apocalypse wins,
　23
Catholics: criticize *Seven Storey
　Mountain,* 31; "ghetto mentality"
　of, 40, 126; thinkers, 80; role in
　twentieth century, 125; and true
　Catholicism, 125–26, 136, 146
censorship: within Roman Catholic
　Church, 10; of *Seven Storey Moun-
　tain,* 22
Chardin, Teilhard de. *See* Teilhard
　de Chardin, Pierre
charity: compared to gentlemanli-
　ness, 4; must be fashioned by Jesus
　Christ, 48; spontaneous, 49; fruit
　of Christian empathy, 49; of Jesus
　Christ, 72
Chicago, Ill.: World's Fair of, 9;
　mentioned by Merton, 33
China: Red treatment of Cistercians
　in, 19, 72; Jesuits in, 127
Chinese, 91
Chinese rites of the mass, 137

Christian ethics: in world affairs, 40,
　70; corruption of, 79, 80; of love,
　88, 94
Christian Failure, The, 82
Christian faith, 45
Christian family: compared to Tao-
　ist plan, 141; criticized, 146
Christian forebears, 79
Christianity: need for asceticism in,
　10; Christian life, 61; true, 68;
　Marx's rejection of, 69; and Com-
　munism, 70–72; threat to, 72, 81;
　crusade, 87; Negro's loss of faith
　in, 110
Christian nonviolent resistance, 114–
　15, 123
Christian perspective, 94
Christian reason, 77
Christians: called upon to renounce
　the world, 27, 28; must influence
　policies in West, 41; tempted away
　from task, 44; cannot separate
　faith and works, 52; must help
　provide human needs, 52; against,
　54; mark is love for mankind, 70;
　Conquistidores, 71; morally para-
　lyzed, 81; duty of, 86; must pre-
　serve life, 86; armies, 89; peace-
　makers, 92; behind iron curtain,
　93; and ammunition factories, 96,
　123; on race, 102; must love fel-
　lowman, 134
Christian theology, 80, 127
Christian west, 90, 93
Chuang Tzu, 139–40
church. *See* Roman Catholic Church
churches of Greece, Russia, the Ori-
　ent, 126
churchmen, 66
Church of England: Merton bap-
　tized into, 1; devoted to, 3; dis-
　appointed in, 3. 4
Cistercian Order: treatment by Chi-
　nese Communists, 19; Asian mem-
　bers visited by Merton, 25; true
　Communists, 70; monks like Zen
　monks, 138–39
citizenship (U.S.), 38
city, metaphor of, 54–58
City of God: book, 10; and man,
　45, 57
Civil Rights Bill of 1964, 106
civil rights movement: successful
　marches of, 103; congressional vic-
　tories for, 103; Merton pessimistic
　about, 106, 108–10
Civil War, 73
classical Rome, 5

Cleaver, Eldridge, 111
cloister, 49, 98
cold war: ethics of, 79, 85; religion for, 87–88, 91; Merton's tendency to oversimplify, 113; mentioned, 67, 75, 78, 99
The Columbian, 8
Columbia University: Merton enters, 6; meets first Communists at, 6; influence on Merton, 7–8; graduate program in English, 9, 135
common life, 59, 138
communism: Merton's admiration for, 6; at Columbia, 6; Merton disappointed in, 7; and Christianity, 70–72
communist: world, 67; saviors, 68; sympathizers, 79; takeover, 80; movements, 119
community: effect on Merton of monastic, 16; contemplative, 30; true, 45; metaphor of the Community, 54, 58–61; the American, 61
concentration camps, 76
Confucianism, 136
Confucius, 127, 141
Conjectures of a Guilty Bystander, 83
Constantinople, 71
contemplation: Merton's life of, 25; Merton's theology of, 31, 46–47; for self-knowledge, 46; helps men communicate, 47; leads to social action, 47; basis for humanism, 47; helps one renounce his empirical self, 48; leads to different view of Church, 48–49; and social action, 51; not just for monks, 51; society with and without, 55; difficult in City, 55; principal task of monk, 62. *See also* contemplative life
contemplative life: happiness in, 28; as Christian vocation, 29; first discussion of, 29; social involvement of, 29, 31; spokeman for, 44; for laymen, 45; not separate from world, 50; meaning of flight from world, 51
Crusaders, 71
Cuban missile crisis, 40
Cuban pilgrimage, 12
Cuban revolution, 73

Dalai Lama, The, 25
Dante: Merton's favorite poet, 6; condemns do-gooders, 48; influence upon Merton, 147

Daughters of the American Revolution, 38
Delp, Alfred, 116
desert: discussed, 50–51; fathers, 63
Detroit riots, 111
dialogue, 63, 114; ecumenical, 125
diaspora, 61–64, 134
A Different Drummer, 103
Divine Comedy, The, 147
Doctor Zhivago, 68
do-gooder, 48
Doherty, Catherine de Huech, 14, 99
Dominicans, 53; theology of, 113
Don Quixote, 70
Douglas, Frederick, 100
Douglaston, Long Island: grandparents' home in, 2; religious education in, 2; Merton's visits to, 5, 8; description of, 8
Duke of Burgandy, 40
Dunne, Dom Frederic: Merton's first abbot, 17; appeals to, for more solitude, 18; strict administration of, 35

early Merton, 27, 33
East and West, 52, 74, 93, 99, 114, 117, 135
Eastern thought, 125
ecumenical dialogue, 47
Eichmann, Adolf, 94
Eliot, T. S., 4
Elman, Paul, 15
"Emperor's New Clothes," 39
empirical "I", 142
England, 3, 6
Enlightenment, 20
Episcopal Church, 2, 5
Establishment, 64, 69, 108, 111
Ethiopia, Merton protests action in, 7
Europe, 72
ex cathedra, 84
existentialism, 130
extermination camps, 108–9
eye-for-an-eye, 123
Ezekiel, book of, 74

"Fable for a War," 11
Faith and Violence, 112
fallout shelters, 78
fanatics, 72
fascism, 87
fatalism, 82
Federal District Court (Louisville, Ky.), 38–39
fellowman, 37, 51
fellow monks: Merton could talk little with, 16; not philosophical, 21;

Merton finds solitude with, 32; like fellow intellectuals, 39
Fenelon, 40–41
First Crusade, 128
first-strike attacks, 78
first vows, 21
Flushing, Long Island, 2
Fox, Dom James: explains treatment of Merton, 19; leads in reforming Gethsemani, 36
Franciscan Order: Merton applies for membership in, 12; Merton rejected by, 12, 53
Franco, Francisco, 7
free world, 67
French Revolution, 62
Friendship House, 14

Galileo, 85
Gandhi, Mahatma, 99, 104, 114; able to synthesize East and West, 116; like a saint to Merton, 117; ideas for Christian to accept, 118–23; Merton studied, 135
gentlemanliness, 4
Geography of Lograire, 108–9
Germany, Merton visits in 1932, 4, 77
Gethsemani Abbey: Merton first hears about, 12; first impression of, 13–14; effect on career, 16; place for Merton to win sainthood, 17; new challenge facing, in 1940s, 17; Merton's desire to leave, 18; Merton's life in, 21–25, 147; Merton's funeral and burial at, 26; new books from, 27; Easter retreat of 1941 described, 28; liberalization in 1950s, 35; and Martin Luther King, 111; helped Merton gain unity, 145
Gilson, Etienne, 10
God: man who loves, 4; presence of, 11; Merton's promise to, 12; union with, 12; bearing soul to, 12; friendship of, 14; word of, to Zachariah, 14; and Merton's need for solitude, 18; glory of, 19; and the world, 23; what He wanted Merton to do, 25; called to Gethsemani by, 26; spirit of, 30; common desire for, 32; kingdom of, 34, 38; sovereign, 34; sees as, 37; gives thanks to, 38; servant of, 41; more perfect way of serving, 43; side of, 44; original creation of, 45; City of, 45, 58; message of, 46; will of, 46; author of man's ex-

istence, 46; possesses secret of identity, 46; temple of, 46; communicates with, 47, 50; met, 47; devoted to, 48; became man in Christ, 48; pleasing to, 49; nauseated, 49; belonging to, 50; find others in, 50–51; society with, 51; love for, 51; each man in, 51; contemplation of, 52, 145; called to monastery by, 52; image of, 54, 71; care not for, 54; rain gift of, 54–55; place to worship, 59; working with, 60; servants of, 62; search for, 63; doctrine of will of, 68; father of Jesus Christ, 68; false definition of, 68; as "out there," 70; of absolute future, 70; wrath of, 70; as builder of better world, 71; kingdom of, 71; love of, 81; the Creator, 86, 96; mocking of, 90; Dante lead to, by Beatrice, 147
Gog and Magog, 74–76
Golden Book Award of Catholic Writers Guild, *The Ascent to Truth* wins in 1951, 23–24
gospel, 72, 83, 116, 121
Graham, Billy, 29
great knowledge, 140
Great Synthesizer, 127, 135
Greenwich Village, 8
guerrilla warfare, 111
"guilty bystander," 28

Hanh Nhat, 138
Harlem: Merton considers working in, 14–15, 17; in poem, 56–57, 99
hawkish chaplains, 85
health: tendency to delicate, 17; loss of, 21, 23; affected by harsh rule, 36
Hearst papers, 6
heaven, 45; of separate individuals, 50, 147
Hemingway, Ernest, 4
hermitage: Merton requests, in 1947, 20; description of, 25; found symbolically in fellow monks, 32; Trappist, 64; Merton's, 66
hieratic gestures, 63
Hindus, 121–22
Hiroshima, atomic attack on, 35, 81, 95
holier-than-thou pose, 44
holiness, 52
Holy Land, 128
Honest to God, 131–33
hope, in racial crisis, 103

Hopkins, Gerard Manley: Merton discovers, 4; chooses as dissertation topic, 11
"The Hot Summer of Sixty-Seven," 106
"How It Is—Apologies to an Unbeliever," 129, 134
human dignity, 53
humanism: based on contemplation, 47, 68, 74; Greek form of, 127
humanitarianism, flaccid, 67
humanity, Merton's renewed love for, 37
hunters (and monks), 35
hybris, 79
hydrogen bomb, 83

idealists, 124
image: "Seven Storey Mountain," 23–24; of world hater, 25; Merton's public, 27, 31; false self, 44, 53; falsity caused by the City, 55
Imitation of Christ. See Thomas à Kempis, Saint
incarnation: doctrine of, 42, 48; logos of, 86, 97
India, 75; partition of, 117–18
Indian Central America, 71
Indians: American, 73, 107, Asian, 119
Indonesia, 75
"Inferno," 147
inner strength, 122
insects, 75
intellectuals: responsible for guarding truth, 39; Merton courted, 64; like monks, 64
"In the Ruins of New York," 56–57
Ionesco, 60–61
iron curtain, 79, 93
Israel, 118
"Is the World a Problem?": Merton attempts to break early stereotype in, 33
I-Thou relationship, 144
ivory-spire philosophers, 124

Jagerstatter, Franz, 116
Janus, 74
Japan, 77, 95
Jester, 8
Jesuit missionaries in China, 127, 136–37, 146
Jesus Christ: devotion to, 12; way to follow, 15; resurrection of, 19; of the burnt men, 26; flame of, 29; way of, 34; one with, 54; society of men without, 58; no room for,

60; victory of, 69; Lordship of, 70; science-oriented to, 70; death of, 71; self-sacrifice of, 71; sentimental and athletic, 74; and the poor, 76; prince of peace, 91; in tradition of, 92; advent of, 103; suffering of, 104, 120; world of, 104; as Lord of History, 104; and the Sermon on the Mount, 115; crucifixion of, 118; eastern epiphany of, 118; the Stranger, 118, 128; and Gandhi, 121; God in, 129; as the Suffering Servant, 129; as Man for others, 131; redemption of, 134; as God's most definitive expression, 137; name of, 143
Jews, 47, 94
John of the Cross, Saint: discussed in *The Ascent to Truth,* 31; Merton's study of, 42; and Bishop Robinson, 132; mentioned, 33
Johnson, President Lyndon B., 40
John XXIII, Pope: leads reform of church, 41; writes *Pacem in Terris,* 41, 96; calls for Catholic involvement in world, 42, 126–27, 135; influence on Merton, 41–42; on war, 84, 96–97; writes *Ad Petri Cathedram,* 91
"Journal of My Escape from the Nazis," 11
Joyce, James, 4, 120
Ju school, 141–42
just war: doctrine of, 80–81, 84, 87; need for reinterpretation, 89

kairos, 103–6
Kelly, William Melvin, 103
Kennedy, President John F.: inaugural address praised, 40; assassination of, 115
Kierkegaard, Soren, 130
killer ape, 115
King, Martin Luther, 99, 103, 104, 111, 114, 116, 122, 123
knobs of Kentucky, 27
koan, 143
Kremlin, 6
Kung Tzu. *See* Confucius

Lao Tzu, 140
later Merton, 27, 33
Latin America, 75
Lawrence, D. H., 4
Leningrad, 85
Lepp, Ignace, 82
"Letter to an Innocent Bystander," 39
"Letter to a White Priest," 102

"Letter to Pablo Antonio Cuadra Concerning Giants," 74
liberalism, 62; nineteenth-century, 67; in northern legislature, 108; thought, 109
Lissner, Will, 8
Little Flower. *See* Therese of Lisieux, Saint
Lord's Prayer, The, 2
Louis, Brother, 15, 18
Louis XIII, King of France, 40
Louisville, Ky.: corruption in, 28; visit in 1948 to, 36; mystical experience in, 37; mentioned, 14, 33
Luther, Martin, 8

Machiavelli, 142
Machiavellian policies, 96–97
manual labor, 138
manuscripts, Greek, Roman, Arabic, 127
March on Washington (1963), 107
Marion Griswald Van Rensselaer Annual Poetry Prize, Merton wins, 11
Maritain, Jacques, 8, 10
Marty, Martin, 108–10
Marx, Karl: mentioned in *Seeds of Contemplation,* 31; Merton agrees with, 67; false prophet, 69
Marxism, 69; effect on the church, 70
Marxists: pervert Marx's teachings, 68; and Christians in dialogue, 130–31
"Marxist Theory and Monastic Theoria," 26
mass media, 80, 98
mass movements, 70–71
mass murder, 84
master of the Choir Novices (1955–1965), Merton as, 23, 24
Master of the Scholastics (1951–1955): Merton as, 24, 32
Mater et Magistra, 52
Mazzolari, Don Primo, 76
Memphis, Tenn., 111
Meng Tzu, 141
Mennonites, 80
Merton, John Paul, 2
Merton, Owen: deserted by Thomas Merton, 1; occupation of, 2; as painter, 2; takes Thomas Merton to France, 3; death of, 3; seems near Merton in Rome, 5
Merton, Ruth Jenkins: described, 1; death of, 2
Middle Ages: hegemony of, 61; Christianity in, 62, 64; commit-

ment in, 88; Christ the Stranger in, 128, 146
military draft, Merton's first attitude toward, 12–13
military leaders, danger of, 95
millennium, 69, 90
Mississippians, 110
Mohammed, 105
Molotov cocktails, 110
monasticism, 62; of the heart, 63
monastic life, superior to life in world, 44
monastic responsibility, Merton's opinion of, in early days, 30
monastic seclusion: Merton's belief in, 28; as a hideaway, 78
monastic vocation, 27, 29; Merton's, 50
monastic volunteers, decline in number of, 43
money changers, 75
monk as example, 51
Monte Alban, 59
moral clichés, 79
Mount Athos, 59
Mountauban, France, lycee in, 3
Muslim, 129
Mystics and Zen Masters, 136
myth of the Good against the Bad, 93

National Catholic Reporter, 109
National Commission on Causes and Prevention of Violence, 98
nationalism, 92–94
National Students League: Merton joins, 7; helps picket Casa Italiana, 7; Merton questioned about, when naturalized, 38
national suicide, 79
natural law, doctrine of, 89
"Nature and Art in William Blake," 10
Naumann, Bernd, 110
Nazis, 82, 93, 110, 116
Nazism: America seemed ready for, in 1968, 76–77; America type of, 102, 109; parades of, 132
Neant, 130
Negro: ghettos, 100, 106; America and, 100–102; rights of, 101; as potential Catholic converts, 102; hour of destiny for, 104; spiritual earnestness of leaders, 105; African strength, 105; nonviolent leadership, 106; tougher leadership, 106; and violence, 110; lost faith in

Christianity, 110; mentioned, 14, 73, 77
neo-Platonism, synthesis with, 127
Nestorians, 105
The New Man, 129
the new morality, 132
new nations, emergence of, 52
New Year's Eve meditation (1950), 34
New York City: Merton agrees to work in Friendship House, 14; sees as Plato's Cave, 37; mentioned, 33, 54, 85, 147
New Zealand, 1, 2
"Nhat Hanh Is My Brother," 138
Niebuhr, H. Richard, 34
Niebuhr, Reinhold, 113
Nietzche, Friedrich, 120
"Night Spirit," 142
No Man Is an Island, shows change in Merton's attitude toward the world, 32
non-Christian, 50, 63–64, 79, 137
noncombatant objector, 13
nonconformist, 66
nonviolence, Christian, 88–90
nonviolent resistance: described, 114–115, 123; misunderstood by Americans, 115
Northern Hemisphere, 75
"Notes on the Future of Monasticism," 51
nuclear war, 52; possibilities and evils of, 77–97; pope's failure to condemn, 83–85; purely spiritual witness against, 87; immorality of, 96, 99, 114
nuclear weapons, 87

Oakham School, The: Merton enters, 3; description of, 4
Occident, 116
October Revolution, 14
optimism, 78, 96
Orient: ill-fated trip to, 47, 137–38; being rebuilt like the West, 144
Original Child Bomb, 95
Oswald, Lee Harvey, 115
otherworldliness, 28, 31
outlaw, 73
oversimplification, Merton's tendency toward, 113
The Oxford Pledge, Merton takes, 7
"Ox Mountain Parable," 141–42

Pacem in Terris. See John XXIII, Pope

pacifism, 7; Christian, 78; conventional not effective, 86; relative, 88; false image of, 89; Gandhi's, 118
papacy, 95
"Paradiso," 147
Paris, France, 1, 2, 3
Pasternak, Boris, 68
patron saint, Merton as, 148
Paul, Saint, 137
Pax, 65; medal given by, 86
peace: movements, 82; strike, 96
Peale, Norman Vincent, 29
Pearl Harbor, Japanese attack on, 15
pessimism: Merton's, much like Camus, 21; in analysis of man's world, 28
Peter, Saint, 137
pilgrimage, 34, 128; to the East, 132
Pius XII, Pope, 84, 92
Plato's Cave, 37
Plotinus, 140
Poland, blitzkrieg of, 84
popes' failure to condemn nuclear war, 83–85
post-Christian era, 77
poverty, and the void, 48
Prades, France, 1
prayer: at Ripley Court School, 3; mental, 31; in *The Ascent to Truth,* 31, 91–92
"Pray for Peace," 90
prison of selfhood, 46, 50, 52
prophet: Merton as, 52
Prophet, The, 57–58
Protestantism: theology of, 56; thinkers in, 80; influence of, on childhood, 125; and Merton, 131; wall between Catholicism and, 134; mentioned, 5, 20, 47
pseudo-angel, 50
"Purgatorio," 147
purgatory, 19
Puritans, 34
Pyrenees Mountains, 1

Quakers: Merton attended services of, 1; disappointed in, 5; protest war, 80

race, 52; war, 99; Merton's tendency to oversimplify, 113
Rahner, Karl, 61, 64
rain, 54–55
"Rain and the Rhinoceros," 54–55
Raphael, 57–58
rationality, climate of, 92
red-hot coals, 105

Red menace, 72
Red Square, 6
Reformation, 62, 127–28
religious specialists, 45
The Review, 8
revivalists of nineteenth century, 34
revolution, spiritual, not social, 29
"right mind," 119
right of self-defense, 84
Ripley Court School, 3
Robert, Dom (Merton's teacher), 17
Robinson, John A. T., 131–34
Roman Catholic Church: family prejudiced against, 2, 5; sacraments of, 3, 8; Merton's conversion to, 10–11; censorship in, 10; in Latin America, 12; influence on Merton, 20; Merton's importance to, 20; witness in Asia of, 25–26; Merton's influence on, 27; believes in power of love, 83; losing influence among blacks, 102; Merton calls for support of civil rights movement from, 110; and non-Christian bodies, 125; in the modern world, 125–28; Italian elements in, 136; should stress experience of faith more, 144
Roman Catholicism. *See* Roman Catholic Church
Rome, Merton visits, in 1933, 4–5
Rorschach ink blots, 95
Russia: movies, 6; monks from, 63, 72, 74, 77; atheistic, 79, 86–87

sacraments. *See* Roman Catholic Church
Saint Antonin, France, 3
Saint Bonaventure's College (Orlean, N.Y.): Merton teaches at, 12; Merton decides to become monk while at, 14; mystical experience at, 15
sainthood: desire for, leads Merton to Gethsemani, 16–17; to achieve, 19; requires involvement in human affairs, 42, 43
Salve Regina, 15
Samson, 105
Sartre, Jean-Paul, 130
scapegoat, 80
scholastic philosophers, 127
second baptism, 16
secular city, 56
Secular Journal of Thomas Merton, The, 14–15
Seeds of Contemplation, Merton shows little social concern in, 30
Seeds of Destruction, 108

seeing, act of, 143
self-analysis, 66
Seven Storey Mountain, The: tells of Merton's decision to work in Harlem, 14; happy ending of, 20; Merton's writing of, personal criticism of, 23–24; seems to predict death, 26; influence in creating the Merton image, 27; describes initial experience at Gethsemani, 28; mentioned, 129
sharecropper, Negro, 103
Sheen, Fulton, 29
Shoshonean Indians, 99
sign language in Abbey, 16
Sign of Jonas, The: shows Merton's dissatisfaction with Gethsemani, 18; reveals his changing attitude toward the world, 32; reveals conclusions about his decision to become a monk, 43
silence, 49
Siloe, the waters of, 29–30
Simeon Stylites, 8
slavery to money and machines, 67
Smith, Alfred E., 40
social action, fruit of contemplation, 48
social commentator, 32, 48
social ethics, 44–52
social gospel, 34
social institutions, 67
socialism, 7
social justice, 67
solemn vows, 22
solitude, 49, 51
Sophocles, 104
Sortais, Dom Gabriel, 36
Soul on Ice, 111
South, 72; pool of potential Catholic converts, 102
Southern Hemisphere, 75
Soviet: forced labor camps, 68; propaganda, 90
Spain, Christian flag of, 136, 146
Speculator, The: Communists control, 6; Merton writes for, 8
Spirit of God, 30
Spirit of Medieval Philosophy, The, 110
Strange Islands, 45
strength of heart, 121
superpowers, 75
Supreme Being, 144
Swift, Frank, Merton's Communist party pseudonym, 7
syncretism, 140

Tammany Hall, 2, 5
Taoism, 139–41
Teilhard de Chardin, Pierre, 70; study of Marx and Engels, 140
Teiresias, 113
Test Ban Treaty of 1963, 77
Theater of the Absurd, 60
Therese of Lisieux, Saint, Merton's prayer to, 15–16
Third World, 75
Thomas, 58
Thomas à Kempis, Saint, 10
Thomas Merton Reader, A, 21
Thoreau, Henry David, 33
Tibetan monks, 26
Tillich, Paul, 131
Time magazine, 95
totalitarianism, 71: in America, 108; and Messianism, 118
Tower of Babel, 54
"Tower of Babel, A Morality," 57–58
Trappists: of Tré Fontane, 5; Merton first hears of, 12; makes Easter retreat with, 13; desires to become member of, 14–15; change in policy of, 17; hold Merton against his wishes, 18; Merton's history of Order of, 29–30; liberalization in 1950s of, 35; decline in membership of, 43, 53
Tré Fontane, 5
Trent: era of, 126; Council of, 127, 146; mentality of, 127
triumphalism, 62
T.V. westerns, 116
two worlds, 53

Ulysses, 120
United Nations, 78, 93
unity, theme of, 145–46
unsuccess, value of, 8
urbanites, 55, 64

Van Doren, Mark, 9
Vatican II: more openness because of, 25; influence on Merton, 41; Merton's letter to bishops at, 82; meaning of, 126–27, 129, 134, 137, 146; progressives at, 135
Versailles, France, 40
Viet Cong, 111–12
Viet Nam: Lyndon Johnson's handling of war in, 40, 56, 92; and violence at home, 98; war in, 111–12, 137, 138

violence: American, 98–99, 115; white collar, 98
vow of stability, 18

Walsh, Daniel: leads Merton to join RCC, 11; suggests Merton join Trappists, 12–13
war: Merton's attitude toward, in 1940, 13; root of, 80–81; overkill in, 98
Waugh, Evelyn, 4
Way of Chuang Tzu, The, 139
weapons: chemical, bacteriological, and nuclear, 81; thermonuclear, 90
Weil, Simone, 116
white conservatives, 106–7
white liberals, 107–8, 113
white man: blamed for American racial crisis, 99; make slaves of darker men, 100; desires punishment, 101; response to black violence, 102; pocketbook of, 102; redemption of, 105
white middleclassdom, 108
womb of collective society, 46
Word, Incarnate, requires followers to work in world, 42
world: disillusionment with, 16; concern for, 27; Merton's changing attitude toward, 27–43; contemplative's relation to, 31; rejection of, 32; Merton's re-evaluation of relationship to, 32; renunciation of, 44; life in, contrasted with life in cloister, 45; distorted parody of God's creation, 45; contempt for, 49; escape from, 52, 66; Merton's attitude toward, 53; to be rejected, 53; of mass man, 53; of imprisoned man, 54; openness to, 54; Community, 61; love affair with, 66; people of, 67; absence from, 67; leaders of, 79
world state, 93
World War I, 1, 62, 73
World War II, 67, 73, 80, 82, 94, 109, 126

"Yankee go home," 73
Young Communist League, 7

Zachariah, 14
Zen Buddhism: Merton interested in, 8, 25; visit with Tibetan Buddhists, 25; values for Catholicism, 142–44
Zen monks, compared to Cistercians, 138–39
zoology, 56